box BY box

JIM STACK

POPULAR WOODWORKING BOOKS
CINCINNATI, OHIO
www.popularwoodworking.com

read this important safety notice

To prevent accidents, keep safety in mind while you work. Use the safety guards installed on power equipment; they are for your protection. When working on power equipment, keep fingers away from saw blades, wear safety goggles to prevent injuries from flying wood chips and sawdust, wear hearing protection and consider installing a dust vacuum to reduce the amount of airborne sawdust in your woodshop. Don't wear loose clothing, such as neckties or shirts with loose sleeves, or jewelry, such as rings, necklaces or bracelets, when working on power equipment. Tie back long hair to prevent it from getting caught in your equipment. People who are sensitive to certain chemicals should check the chemical content of any product before using it. The authors and editors who compiled this book have tried to make the contents as accurate and correct as possible. Plans, illustrations, photographs and text have been carefully checked. All instructions, plans and projects should be carefully read, studied and understood before beginning construction. In some photos, power tool guards have been removed to more clearly show the operation being demonstrated. Always use all safety guards and attachments that come with your power tools. Due to the variability of local conditions, construction materials, skill levels, etc., neither the author nor Popular Woodworking Books assumes any responsibility for any accidents, injuries, damages or other losses incurred resulting from the material presented in this book. Prices listed for supplies and equipment were current at the time of publication and are subject to change. Glass shelving should have all edges polished and must be tempered. Untempered glass shelves may shatter and can cause serious bodily injury. Tempered shelves are very strong and if they break will just crumble, minimizing personal injury.

metric conversion chart

to convert	to	multiply by
Inches	Centimeters	2.54
Centimeters	Inches	0.4
Feet	Centimeters	30.5
Centimeters	Feet	0.03
Yards	Meters	0.9
Meters	Yards	1.1

Distributed in Canada by Fraser Direct
100 Armstrong Avenue
Georgetown, Ontario L7G 5S4
Canada

Distributed in the U.K. and Europe by David & Charles
Brunel House
Newton Abbot
Devon TQ12 4PU
England
Tel: (+44) 1626 323200
Fax: (+44) 1626 323319
E-mail: mail@davidandcharles.co.uk

Distributed in Australia by Capricorn Link
P.O. Box 704
Windsor, NSW 2756
Australia

Visit our Web site at www.popularwoodworking.com for information on more resources for woodworkers.

Other fine Popular Woodworking Books are available from your local bookstore or direct from the publisher.

10   09   08   07   06   5   4   3   2   1

Library of Congress Cataloging-in-Publication Data

Stack, Jim, 1951-
    Box by box / Jim Stack.
        p.   cm.
    Includes index.
    ISBN-13: 978-1-55870-774-0 (hardcover: alk.paper)
    ISBN-10: 1-55870-774-3 (hardcover: alk. paper)
    1. Woodwork.   2. Wooden boxes.   I. Title.
TT200.S68   2006
684.'08--dc22   2005035723

ACQUISITIONS EDITOR: Jim Stack
EDITOR: Amy Hattersley
DESIGNER: Brian Roeth
TECHNICAL ILLUSTRATOR: Jim Stack
PROJECT PHOTOGRAPHER: Al Parrish
PRODUCTION COORDINATOR: Jennifer L. Wagner

F+W PUBLICATIONS, INC.

PHOTO: BRIAN STACK

about the author

Jim Stack worked in commercial cabi-
net- and furniture-making shops for 16
years and ran his own furniture-making
shop for 5½ years (that half a year is very
memorable, so it's important to include
it). For the past 6+ years, he's been the
acquisitions editor for Popular Woodworking Books.

When Jim's not cutting wood he's cut-
tin' up in the woods — usually on his
mountain bike.

Jim is the author of *Northwoods Furniture, The Biscuit Joiner Project Book,
Design Your Own Furniture, Building
the Perfect Tool Chest* and *Cutting-Edge
Router Tips & Tricks*.

acknowledgements

Thanks to those who helped in the making of this book. Most of you know who
you are. For those of you who don't, that's
OK. I know who you are and I appreciate
your time and advice.

Many thanks to editor Amy Hattersley
(who was patient with my many changes
to the manuscript and layout), book designer Brian Roeth (who was also patient
with my many changes to the manuscript
and layout), chapter opener photographer
Al Parrish (whose photos add credibility
to my projects and kicked up the artistic
level of this book several notches), photo
stylist Nora Martini (who supplied the
props and set up the chapter opener photos) and production coordinator Jennifer
Wagner (who gathered all the book stuff
together and made it possible for this
book to actually be printed).

To my wife and best friend, Gina, (who
was patient with several months of box
building in our basement and later, storage of those boxes in our dining room).

To my three adult children Brian, Re-
becca and Kelly. Remember that families
are forever!

for the record

I want to make it clear from the outset that I have removed all guards from my power tools so I could show clearly the techniques I'm demonstrating in this book. I also have the tools turned off when showing these procedures.

I do not mean to imply that I use my power tools without their guards. Far from it — I use all the guards all the time and I use them proudly. I've been fortunate to have a good safety record in my career. Aside from the occasional cuts, scratches and abrasions, I've had no major mishaps.

If a particular setup feels wrong or awkward to you, it probably is wrong. Trust your instincts when it comes to power tool usage and setup. A digit saved today is a digit you can use tomorrow. I've grown attached (pun intended) to my fingers and I intend to keep them.

Also, wear eye, ear and breathing protection. This is a pastime that is rewarding and satisfying. Keep yourself safe so you can enjoy it for a lifetime.

Woodworking skill levels for this book are defined as:

■ **basic** | Those folks who are interested in woodworking and know how to use a saw, hammer, screwdriver, drill, possibly a hand plane and sandpaper wrapped around a block of wood. This includes those who have some experience but consider themselves beginners.

■ **intermediate** | Those folks who have been woodworking for a while and have basic knowledge (and hope-fully hands-on experience) using sta-tionary and handheld electric-powered woodworking tools such as a thickness planer, jointer, table saw, router, band saw, jigsaw, random-orbit sander, drill and possibly a lathe and scroll saw. This includes those who consider themselves experienced woodworkers.

■ **advanced** | Those folks who have been woodworking for years and are experienced in all areas of woodwork-ing, including laying up veneers, bending wood, doing inlay work, and they are comfortable using all woodworking tools.

What matters is your confidence as a woodworker. This affects how you ap-proach woodworking and how you feel about your abilities to do the actual work. There are lots of things to consider when woodworking: design, drawing, creating materials lists, making cutting lists and the actual cutting, shaping and working of the wood. Finally, there's the finishing of your projects, which you've spent a lot of time creating.

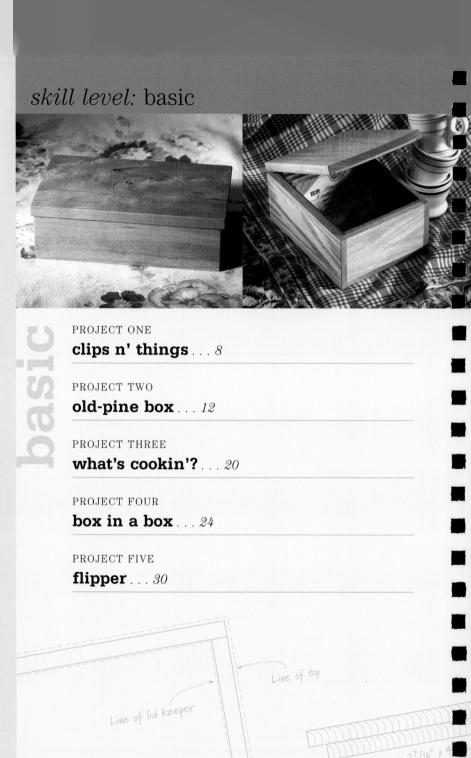

skill level: basic

basic

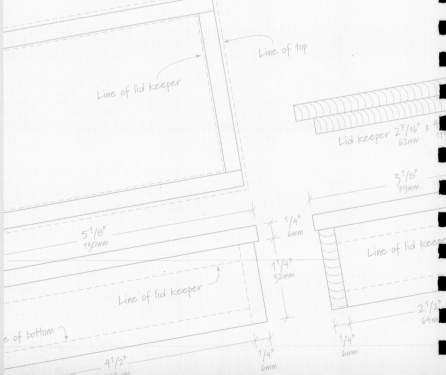

Line of top

Line of lid keeper

Line of lid keeper

Lid keeper 2⁷/16" x 4¹/₂"
62mm   113mm

3¹/8"
79mm

¹/4"
6mm

5¹/8"
130mm

1¹/4"
32mm

Line of lid keeper

Line of lid keeper

2¹/₂"
64mm

Line of bottom

¹/4"
6mm

4¹/₂"

¹/4"
6mm

skill level: *intermediate*

skill level: *advanced*

intermediate

advanced

FOR ALL SEASONS. There are plenty of box ideas in this book. After all, most things are basically boxes. Your house, your car, your room, your computer, your cup, your pencil holder, your purse, King Tut's tomb and of course the most famous box of all, television.

"I want to learn woodworking, so what's the first thing I should make?" I've been asked this question many times, and my answer is always the same — build a box.

That's what this book is about. Building boxes. Each project is graded according to your individual woodworking abilities. If you are a beginning woodworker, start with the first project. After you've built that one, build the second one. And so on. While building each project, you will learn one or more woodworking techniques that will enable you to build the next box. Rest assured, there are projects for any level of woodworker from beginner to advanced.

I know what you're thinking — golly Jim, how many boxes can one person build? Won't you run out of ideas or get bored and beg to watch *Leave it to Beaver* reruns? No, you won't run out of ideas. I've just scratched the surface for box ideas in this book. It's up to you to

put on your Tom Terrific thinking cap and extricate,

expand and extrapolate your own box concepts.

As usual, I've stolen most of the designs contained

in this book and tried to make them my own, so I expect

nothing less from you, my fellow woodworkers. It's all

been done before anyway — just not by you — so go for

it. And finally, keep makin' sawdust.

Jim Stack

clips n' things

FOR SUCH A SIMPLE BOX, it's small and kind of cute, actually. It consists of two sides, two ends, a bottom, a lid and a lid keeper. Simple and sweet. You can keep your paper clips, pushpins, coins, paper money or spitwads in the box.

What you'll learn building this box is how the parts' sizes relate to the overall finished dimensions of the project. You'll see that you need to allow for the thickness of the sides when figuring the length of the ends and allow for the thickness of all the sides when determining the dimensions of the bottom.

It's not uncommon for beginners to cut all the parts of a box to the finished dimensions of the box itself. The builder hurries without stopping to think about how the project is going to be assembled and how the parts relate to each other.

You might be wondering if glue and butt joints are good enough to keep this box together. In a word, yes. When the parts are clamped together, the glue in the joints is forced into the pores of the wood. The glue creates a bridge between the parts. When the glue dries, the bond is strong and will

withstand normal amounts of stress. If the box were to be dropped, it would probably survive intact. I'm not a mathematician, but the odds are in favor of it holding together rather than blasting apart. Of course, if it is thrown on the floor or against a wall, all bets are off.

I don't know what it is about small boxes, but people like them. Give them away as gifts and you'll be showered with compliments. And because these boxes are small, you can use select (really nice) wood without overspending on materials.

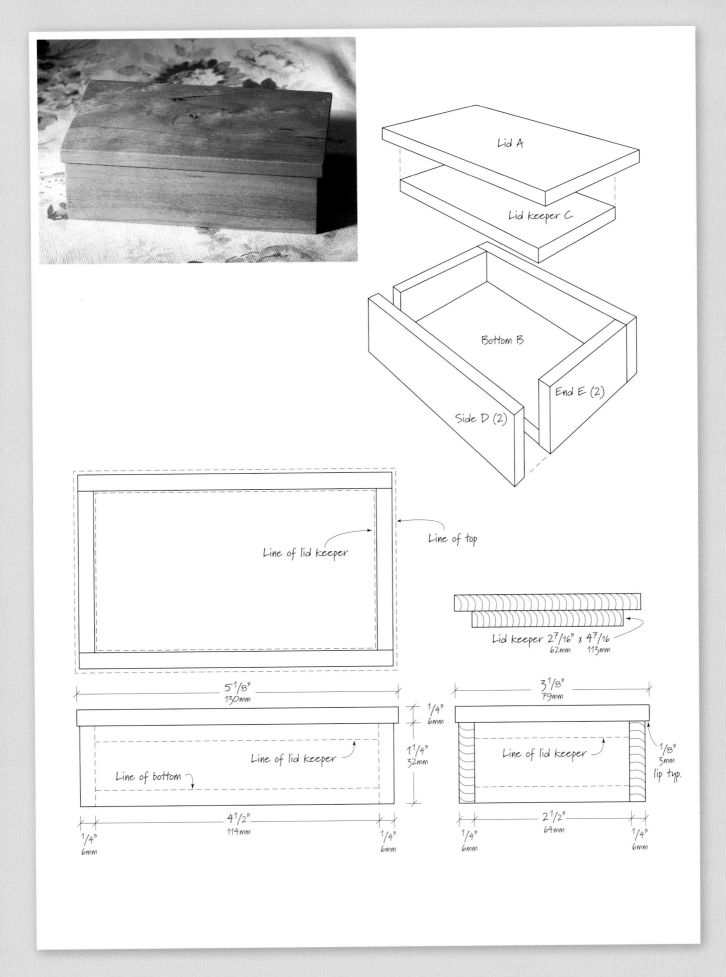

Lid A

Lid keeper C

Bottom B

End E (2)

Side D (2)

Line of lid keeper

Line of top

Line of lid keeper

Lid keeper $2^7/16$" x $4^7/16$
62mm   113mm

$5^1/8$"
130mm

$1/4$"
6mm

$1^1/4$"
32mm

Line of lid keeper

Line of bottom

$4^1/2$"
114mm

$1/4$"
6mm

$1/4$"
6mm

$3^1/8$"
79mm

Line of lid keeper

$1/8$"
3mm
lip typ.

$2^1/2$"
64mm

$1/4$"
6mm

$1/4$"
6mm

inches (millimeters)

REFERENCE	QUANTITY	PART	STOCK	THICKNESS	(mm)	WIDTH	(mm)	LENGTH	(mm)
A	1	top	cherry	1/4	(6)	3 1/8	(79)	5 1/8	(130)
B	1	bottom	cherry	1/4	(6)	2 1/2	(64)	4 1/2	(114)
C	1	lid keeper	cherry	1/4	(6)	2 7/16	(62)	4 7/16	(113)
D	2	sides	cherry	1/4	(6)	1 1/4	(32)	5	(127)
E	2	ends	cherry	1/4	(6))	1 1/4	(32)	2 1/2	(64)

Tools needed

hand saw with miter box

60-, 100-, 120-, 150- and 220-grit sandpapers

No. 0000 steel wool

sanding block (see sanding block sidebar page 11)

block plane (optional)

bench plane (optional)

random-orbit electric sander (optional)

stationary sander (optional)

Hardware & Supplies

spray or wipe-on lacquer

You can use a hand miter saw or power miter saw to cut the parts to size. (See the "Old-Pine Box" project, step 7.) Glue the ends to the bottom. Be sure the edges of all parts are flush with each other.

Glue the sides to the end/bottom assembly. Line up the ends of the sides flush with the end pieces. Wipe away any glue squeeze-out with a damp rag. If you rinse the damp rag frequently, you won't spread the glue around. The clean rag will pick up the glue. The damp rag will wet the wood, which will help you see where excess glue might be lurking.

It's important that you center the keeper on the lid. Measure and mark where the keeper will be located, then apply glue and use spring clamps to hold it in place. Spring clamps are easy to use and inexpensive to purchase.

Use a stationary power sander to sand the ends of the box smooth.

Over the years, I've collected a large arsenal of sanding blocks. The gray ones are made from scrap Homasote®, which is a medium-density material used for pinup boards. It's perfect for sanding blocks used to soften sharp edges. The one on the right has a cork bottom and functions the same as the Homasote®. There's one with a hard rubber bottom for wet sanding, one with a Scotch-Brite® pad on the bottom for contour sanding and several that are formed to specific shapes for sanding mouldings.

Years ago, in one of the shops where I worked, one of the guys showed me a sanding block that he had inserted into a 4" × 24" (102mm × 610mm) sanding belt. I thought it was a great idea. I've had one of these blocks ever since. It's great for leveling and flattening surfaces quickly.

My standard sanding block is ¾" × 3" × 5½" (19mm × 76mm × 140mm). I tear an 8½" × 11" (216mm × 279mm) sheet of sandpaper into fourths (I even made a jig to cut the sandpaper cleanly and straight so I can have a pile of quartered sandpaper in about 30 seconds) and wrap one of these around the block. The part of the sandpaper that wraps up the sides provides a grip to help hold the sandpaper tight against the block and gives good control of the block.

I know what you're thinking — this guy sure is particular about his sanding block! Well, this little guy has sanded miles and miles of edges, flats and whatever else needed sanding. When you're working in a production shop, time is money. I would tear myself a pile of sandpaper and have it standing by, ready. I didn't need to stop and refold the paper, I just grabbed another sheet and kept working. I found that if sandpaper is folded back on itself and used that way, the unused parts become worn because the rough paper is rubbing against itself. Picky? Maybe, but that's just me.

Another method of sanding the box is to use a sanding block wrapped with sandpaper. (In fact, if you used a stationary sander, you'll still need to hand sand.) If you've cut your parts accurately, you won't have much sanding to do. Start with 120-grit sandpaper. Then use 150-grit, then 180-grit. Finish sanding the box using 220-grit sandpaper. Each time you change to a finer grit (the higher the grit number on the sandpaper, the finer or smoother the finish), sand with it until the sanding marks left by the previous grit are removed. Don't try to jump from 120 grit to 220 grit. The 220 grit won't remove the 120 grit's sanding marks easily. When you finish sanding with the 220-grit sandpaper, the surface of the wood will feel super smooth and will have a low-luster sheen. When you apply finish to a surface that has been prepared this way, you will need no more than two coats.

old-pine box

THE WOOD FOR THIS BOX came from my bathroom closet. No, I'm not so desperate that I've started demolishing my house for wood. I was replacing some slightly cupped and ill-fitting painted shelves with something a little flatter and better fitting. The end grain didn't have paint on it, so I knew the wood was some species of pine. I removed five coats of the toughest paint I've ever had to deal with but it was worth it!

I was happy to see that the wood was yellow pine. It was at least 70 years old and had that great, kinda sweet, kinda musty smell that only old wood can have. It was certainly stable in moisture content, so I proceeded immediately, cutting and planing it to the dimensional thickness that I wanted. The rest you'll see in the pictures that follow.

So, find some wood. Go to your local home improvement center or lumberyard and ask for some white pine or yellow pine. White pine is a softer wood that is easier to work than yellow pine because it's softer, is more consistent in grain texture (which means it's easier to sand smooth and level) and it doesn't split as easily. Or, check your closets — there could be some lumber hiding there just waiting for you to give it new life.

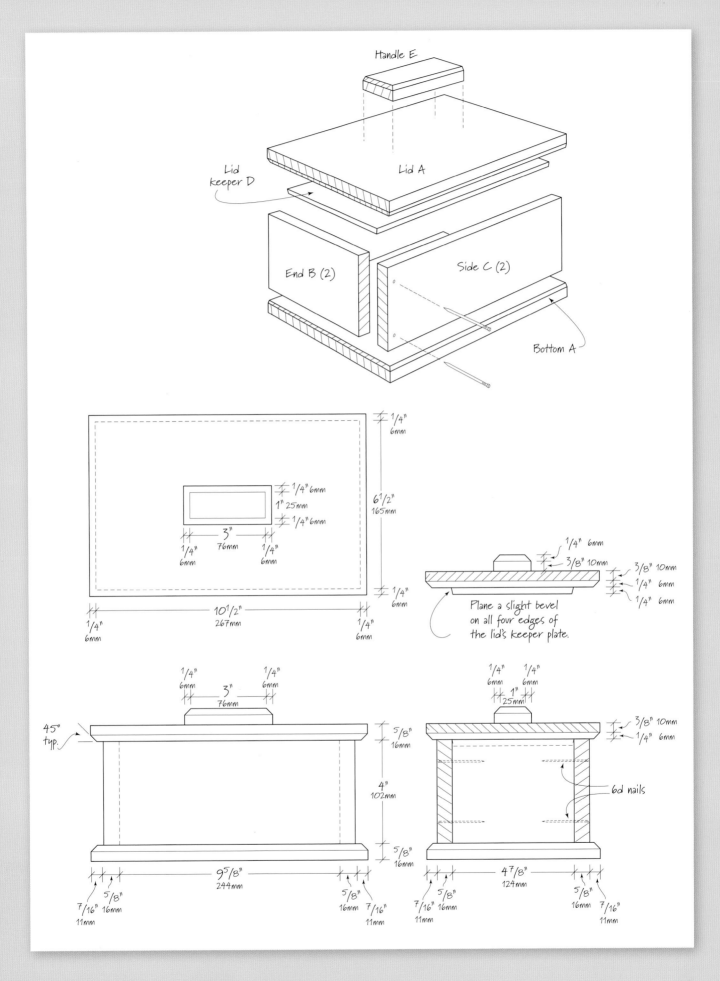

Handle E

Lid A

Lid keeper D

End B (2)

Side C (2)

Bottom A

1/4" 6mm

1/4" 6mm
1" 25mm
1/4" 6mm

6 1/2" 165mm

3" 76mm
1/4" 6mm   1/4" 6mm

10 1/2" 267mm
1/4" 6mm   1/4" 6mm

1/4" 6mm
3/8" 10mm

3/8" 10mm
1/4" 6mm
1/4" 6mm

Plane a slight bevel on all four edges of the lid's keeper plate.

1/4" 6mm   1/4" 6mm
3" 76mm

45° typ.

5/8" 16mm

4" 102mm

5/8" 16mm

9 5/8" 244mm
7/16" 11mm   5/8" 16mm   5/8" 16mm   7/16" 11mm

1/4" 6mm   1/4" 6mm
1" 25mm

3/8" 10mm
1/4" 6mm

6d nails

4 7/8" 124mm
7/16" 11mm   5/8" 16mm   5/8" 16mm   7/16" 11mm

inches (millimeters)

REFERENCE	QUANTITY	PART	STOCK	THICKNESS	(mm)	WIDTH	(mm)	LENGTH	(mm)
A	2	lid and bottom	pine	$5/8$	(16)	7	(178)	11	(279)
B	2	ends	pine	$5/8$	(16)	4	(102)	$4^7/8$	(124)
C	2	sides	pine	$5/8$	(16)	4	(102)	$10^1/8$	(257)
D	1	lid keeper	pine	$1/4$	(6)	$4^7/8$	(124)	$9^5/8$	(244)
E	1	handle	pine	$5/8$	(16)	$1^1/2$	(38)	$3^1/2$	(89)

Hardware & Supplies

10 #8 x $1^1/2$" (38mm) wood screws
8   #6 x $3/4$" (19mm) wood screws
12 6d finish nails
two part epoxy
black paint (or color you like)
amber shellac finish

Tools needed

hand saw with miter box
60-, 100-, 120-, 150- and 220-grit sandpapers
No. 0000 steel wool
sanding block
block plane
bench plane
random-orbit electric sander (optional)

1

If you can find boards about 3" (76mm) to 4" (102mm) wide, that's perfect. Go to your local store and ask for 1 × 4 pine boards. (The actual dimensions of these boards will be $3/4$" × $3^1/2$" [19mm × 89mm].) For the top and bottom parts, you'll need to glue a couple of boards together to get the proper width. As in the photo above, try to match grain patterns from different boards so they blend with each other. While the match in this photos looks OK, you should try different combinations to see if you can get something that looks even better.

2

Voilá! By simply switching the boards left to right, the patterns blend nicely.

3

Sometimes a second opinion is helpful. Izzy thought everything looked good, so that's how we left it.

4

Pipe clamps are inexpensive and will last forever. I've had these clamps for over 20 years and they're still pulling things together. Put some masking tape on the pipe before glue-up. Sometimes glue oozes from the glue joint and runs onto the pipe. This pulls color from the pipe up through the glue and into the wood. It's a difficult stain to sand out, so avoid it.

5

Apply just enough glue to do the job. How much is enough? When the glue is spread over the surface of the joint, it should be a thin film that is slightly transparent.

6

My finger is the best applicator I've found for this type of glue-up. I always have it with me and it's an easy cleanup. The reason for smoothing the glue is to thin it. Then, when the parts are put together, they won't slide around while you clamp. When tightening the clamps, gently tighten one, then go to the next one and so on. Go back to the first clamp and snug it up. Do not tighten until you hear the wood screaming. It's unnecessary work on your part, and the glue will hold without being forced out of the joint. I've seen clamps that are so tight the head of the screw has penetrated the clamp's face. That's just bad joinery.

You'll want the edges of boards that are to be edge-glued to be straight and smooth. Well, Jim, that's nice. How do I do that? Here are some methods you can try.

The first is the time-honored hand planing of the board's edges straight and smooth. This takes practice, but once you get the feel of the plane, it's fun to do.

Another method is to use a stationary power tool called, oddly enough, a jointer. A jointer straightens the edges of boards quickly and accurately.

You can also use a router set up in a router table. Install a straight bit in the router and use a two-part fence that looks like a jointer table turned vertically. The outfeed fence is offset slightly to compensate for the material the router bit removes.

step three | For the final test, put the boards' edges together. There should be no gaps. This process is one that has been used for hundreds of years and is worth learning. Practice, practice, practice!

step one | Use a vise to hold the board. Plane the edge and check for square. Practicing is the only way to get this technique perfect.

step two | Use your eye to check for straitness of the planed edge. Sight down the board and look for a curve or waviness. Replane and check again until it's straight.

photo at right | Using a stationary power jointer isn't difficult. If the fence is square to the bed, you'll make a square edge on the board. If the infeed and outfeed tables are parallel to each other and the outfeed is flush with the cutter's edge, the boards will be straight. Keep the board snug against the fence and run the board's edge over the spinning cutter. A steady feed works well. When the board starts onto the outfeed table, keep light pressure on it. Take as few passes as possible to straighten boards using this tool. Passes eat wood and can dramatically change the dimensional width of your board in short order!

photo at left | You can use a straight bit in a router that is set up in a router table to joint edges straight. It's like using a jointer with its bed sitting vertically. The outfeed fence is offset so it's flush with the cutter's edge. This method works especially well with a straight shear cutting bit because the cutter is angled such that it slices the wood and minimizes grain tear-out. That means it leaves a super-cool clean cut.

7

Here you'll cut the sides and ends for your box to size. I'm using a handsaw called a back saw because it has a stiffening rod attached to its top or back edge. It's mounted in a miter box. I grew up using one of these tools and I love it. If the saw is sharp, you can cut a lot of wood quickly and accurately.

8

Lay out the locations for the nails in the side pieces. When this box is done, the nails' locations will be visible so you might as well space them evenly for a cleaner look. Sometimes seeing where the fasteners are located on a project gives it a solid look and says, "Hey, I used nails to put this box together."

9

Stand the two end pieces on end. Lay one of the side pieces on top of them. Line up the side with one of the ends. Drill pilot holes for the nails. Do this at all four corner joints. If you don't, driving the nails into the unsuspecting wood will cause it to panic and split. Don't surprise your wood, let it know what you're going to do.

10

Use glue and nails to attach the sides to the ends. Then set the finishing nail's heads below the surface of the wood about ⅛" (3mm). A few stout blows with your hammer should do the trick.

Now is the time to sand the side/end assembly. A piece of sandpaper wrapped around a sanding block is another one of those tools that's been used for a long time. It's one of the best ways to smooth and flatten your work. Start with 100-grit sandpaper and work through to 150 grit. You, as the source of power for this tool, can control the rate and pressure of the sanding. I once worked in a shop where we built high-end veneered furniture. Hand sanding was how we evened the veneers, even for large conference tables. Power sanders can sand through veneers in a couple of seconds — it's back to square one when that happens.

Take the boards you glued up out of the clamps. Flatten the surface of these boards using a midsize hand plane called a bench plane. Use a metal ruler as a straightedge to check for flatness. Hold it across, lengthwise and diagonally on the surfaces you're planing to make sure all are straight and flat. If you don't have a plane, you can use 60-grit sandpaper and a flat sanding block to perform this operation. It takes a little longer but it does work! Smooth with finer grits of sandpaper.

Now you get to use a small plane called a block plane. You can use this with one hand and comb your hair with the other hand. Cut bevels on the bottom edges of the top and on the top edges of the bottom. Got that? See the illustration if you have any questions. The size of this bevel is up to you. Stop planing when you think it looks right. Here again, if you don't have a plane, you can use 60-grit sandpaper and your sanding block to make the bevels. Smooth with finer grits of sandpaper.

Use a backer board when cutting the bevels on the end grain. This will prevent splitting the wood at the end of the cut. And we already know how your wood hates to be forced to split.

15

Using the box as a pattern, trace around the inside of it and scribe a line on the bottom of the lid. This line shows you exactly where to locate the keeper. I call it the keeper because it's attached to the underside of the lid and keeps it in place. Duh. Also, you'll notice the screw holes in the bottom of the box. I attached the bottom, then remembered I needed to perform the operation show here. Oops, but no harm, no foul.

17

Measure the inside of the box and cut the keeper just a little larger in both width and length. Use your block plane to fine-tune the fit of the keeper. You want it to fit just shy of snug, but not too shy or the lid will move around. When people remove the lid to look into the box, then replace the lid (and they will because we are all naturally curious), they'll notice how well it fits and will compliment you until it gets embarrassing. Then they'll want you to make them a box that they can open and close in the privacy of their own home. Now back to your box. Center the keeper on the lines you scribed on the underside of the lid. Attach it to the underside of the lid using screws only, no glue. If you glue the keeper to the lid, it could cause the lid to warp because of tension caused by the keeper. Though the screws are firmly in place, the keeper and the lid will be able to expand and contract independently of each other. This will greatly reduce the chances of the lid changing shape.

16

Attach the bottom to the bottom of the box. That makes sense, doesn't it? Predrill for the screws and use a countersink drill bit to cut bevels for the screw's heads. Here I'm using a Yankee screwdriver. As you push up and down on the handle, as if by magic (and it well could be magic), the screwdriver's tip turns and drives the screw into place. This involves no electricity, just power from your arms. Cool. I worked in one shop years ago that issued these screwdrivers to all employees, and we assembled cabinets all day long using them.

18

Remember those nail heads you set? Well, mix up some two-part epoxy, add a few drops of black paint (or pink or orange or whatever you like), mix it a little more and use this mess to fill the nail holes. I know they look bad now, but when you sand the epoxy filler level with the surface of the sides it will look lovely. When the epoxy cures (letting it cure overnight is a good rule to follow), sand the box.

what's cookin'?

WHEN I WENT AWAY TO COL-LEGE, my mother sent copies of all her recipes with me. I still have them and have enjoyed making the food that gave me comfort as a child. This box is made to hold 3" x 5" (76mm x 127mm) note cards. I know a lot of recipe cards are 5" x 7" (127mm x 178mm), so add the necessary dimensions if this is the case with your recipes. Of course, you can use this box as

a jumping-off project to create a series of boxes to hold note cards with secret recipes, notes for your family-history project or your next great novel.

This project is made differently from the previous projects — the sides and ends are glued together, then the top and bottom are attached. This makes a totally enclosed box. The lid is then cut from the assembly. Doing it this way ensures the lid

will fit perfectly and the wood grain will match.

This project demonstrates another way to keep a lid in place. A lip is created by attaching the liner panels inside the box and letting them extend past the top edges of the sides. This gives the lid something to grab on to. I put hinges on this box just make it a little easier to open and close the box without losing the lid.

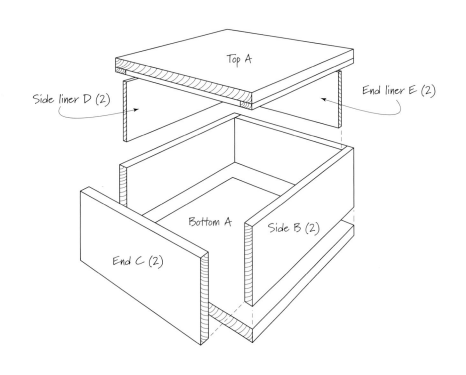

Top A

Side liner D (2)

End liner E (2)

Bottom A

Side B (2)

End C (2)

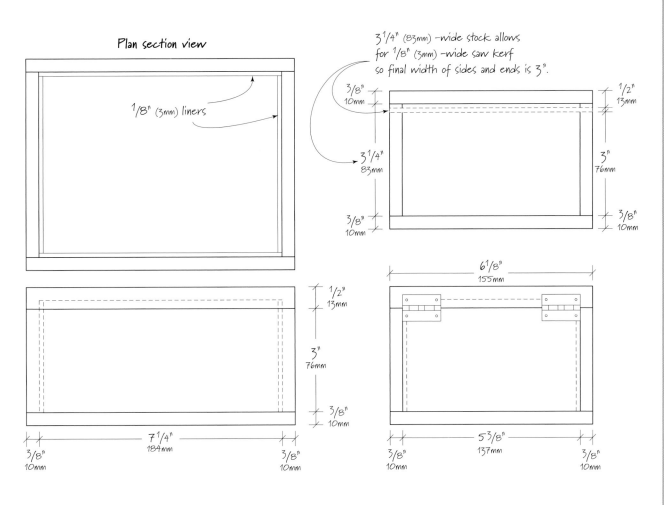

Plan section view

1/8" (3mm) liners

3 1/4" (83mm) -wide stock allows
for 1/8" (3mm) -wide saw kerf
so final width of sides and ends is 3".

3/8"
10mm

1/2"
13mm

3 1/4"
83mm

3"
76mm

3/8"
10mm

3/8"
10mm

1/2"
13mm

3"
76mm

3/8"
10mm

7 1/4"
184mm

3/8"
10mm

3/8"
10mm

6 1/8"
155mm

5 3/8"
137mm

3/8"
10mm

3/8"
10mm

inches (millimeters)

REFERENCE	QUANTITY	PART	STOCK	THICKNESS	(mm)	WIDTH	(mm)	LENGTH	(mm)
A	1	top and bottom	red oak	3/8	(10)	6 1/8	(156)	8	(203)
B	2	sides	red oak	3/8	(10)	3 1/4	(83)	8	(203)
C	2	ends	red oak	3/8	(10)	3 1/4	(83)	5 3/8	(137)
D	2	side liners	red oak	1/8	(3)	3 1/8	(79)	7 1/4	(130)
D	2	end liners	red oak	1/8	(3)	3 1/8	(79)	5 1/8	(130)

Hardware & Supplies

1 pair 1" x 1 1/2" (25mm x 38mm) brass butt hinges

spray or wipe-on lacquer

Tools needed

hand saw with miter box

60-, 100-, 120-, 150- and 220-grit sandpapers

No. 0000 steel wool

sanding block

block plane

bench plane

random-orbit electric sander (optional)

Once you've got the parts cut, lay out the sides and ends. Add glue and clamp the ends between the sides.

Measure the diagonals. When they're equal, the box is square.

When the glue is dry on the end/side assembly, attach the top and bottom parts. You now have a box.

Use a stationary sander or hand sand the box smooth.

5

Cut the lid from the box. The dimensions for the width of the sides and ends in the cutting allow for the width of the saw blade kerf. The box will still be deep enough to hold the 3" × 5" (76mm × 127mm) note cards.

6

Here's how the lid should look. It has a small lip that will match up with the liner sides.

7

Fit the side liners first, then fit the end liners between the side liners. Use your trusty spring clamps to glue the liners in place.

8

When the glue has dried, put the lid on the box, clamp the whole thing together and give it a final sanding.

9

After the finish is applied, you can add hinges if you like. To keep it simple, attach the hinges directly on the back of the box. Now get those recipes organized and start cookin'.

box in a box

WHEN I WAS WORKING ON THIS BOOK, people kept asking me what I put in this box or that box. Sometimes a box is just a box — or in this case, a box in a box.

You'll learn how to install runners for the inner box, drill countersunk holes and use wooden plugs to hide the screw heads.

The bigger box is held together with eight screws and it's strong. I use screws whenever I can — according to famous woodworker Sam Maloof, they're like metal dowels, and I agree. I prefer sheet-metal screws because they have threads the entire length of their shaft, which gives them holding power from top to bottom. Also, their threads aren't as steep as drywall screws, so they pull things together quite nicely.

The design of this box can be adapted to the making of a toolbox or hope chest. The sliding box makes smaller things accessible while larger items are stored below.

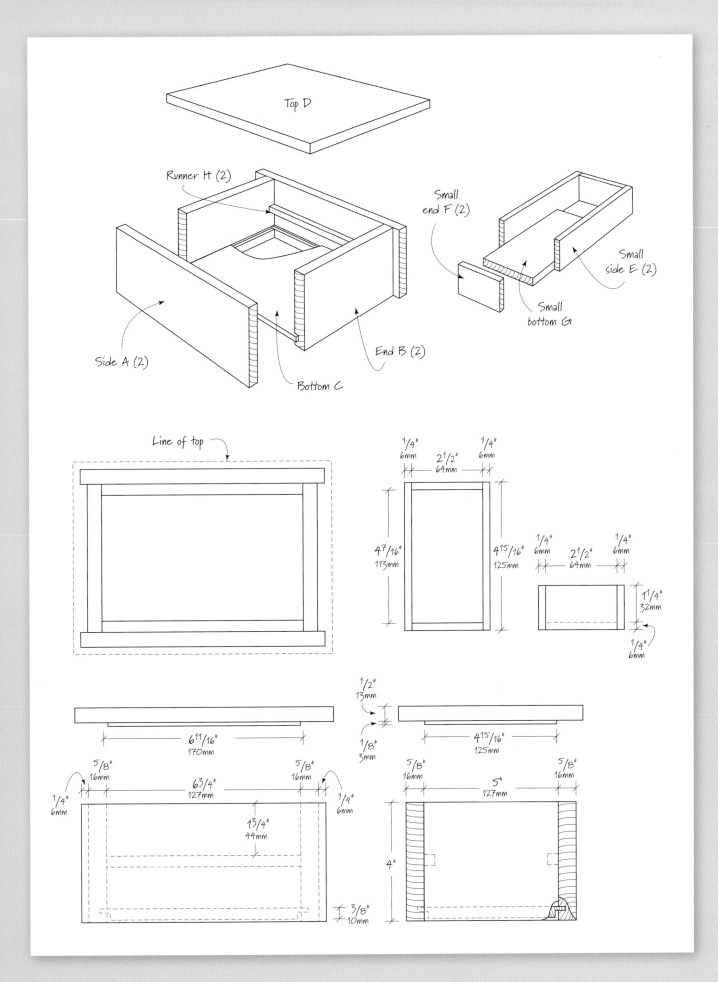

Top D

Runner H (2)

Small end F (2)

Small side E (2)

Side A (2)

Small bottom G

Bottom C

End B (2)

Line of top

1/4" 6mm   2 1/2" 64mm   1/4" 6mm

4 7/16" 113mm

4 15/16" 125mm

1/4" 6mm   2 1/2" 64mm   1/4" 6mm

1 1/4" 32mm

1/4" 6mm

1/2" 13mm

6 11/16" 170mm

1/8" 3mm

4 15/16" 125mm

5/8" 16mm   6 3/4" 127mm   5/8" 16mm

1/4" 6mm   1/4" 6mm

1 3/4" 44mm

5/8" 16mm   5" 127mm   5/8" 16mm

4"

3/8" 10mm

inches (millimeters)

REFERENCE	QUANTITY	PART	STOCK	THICKNESS	(mm)	WIDTH	(mm)	LENGTH	(mm)
A	2	sides	walnut	5/8	(16)	4	(102)	8 1/2	(216)
B	2	ends	walnut	5/8	(16)	4	(102)	5	(127)
C	1	bottom	walnut	3/8	(10)	5 1/4	(133)	7 1/4	(184)
D	1	lid	walnut	5/8	(16)	6 1/2	(165)	9	(229)
E	2	small sides	walnut	1/4	(6)	1 1/2	(38)	4 15/16	(125)
F	2	small ends	walnut	1/4	(6)	1 1/2	(38)	2 1/2	(64)
G	1	small bottom	walnut	1/4	(6)	2 1/2	(64)	4 7/16	(113)
H	2	runners	walnut	3/8	(10)	3/8	(10)	6 3/4	(171)

Tools needed

hand saw with miter box

60-, 100-, 120-, 150- and 220-grit sandpapers

No. 0000 steel wool

sanding block (see sanding block sidebar page 11)

block plane (optional)

bench plane (optional)

random-orbit electric sander (optional)

stationary sander (optional)

Hardware & Supplies

spray or wipe-on lacquer

Cut the box sides and ends, then rout the groove for the bottom. Note the stopped groove in the sides. If you made a through-cut on the sides, the end of the groove would show when the box was assembled.

Cut the rabbet to create the lip on the bottom. Make the first cut holding the bottom vertically against the saw fence. This sets the thickness of the lip. Be sure to make test cuts before cutting the piece from your walnut stock!

Make the second cut to complete the rabbet, which creates the lip on the bottom.

4

Sand the insides of the box prior to assembly.

5

Clamp the sides to the ends. Be sure to install the bottom too! Mark the hole locations so they are evenly spaced. Then drill a pilot hole using a drill bit with a combination twist drill and countersink (this bit is shown below the drill in the photo). Make the countersunk holes about ¼" (6mm) deep.

6

Cut the runners to length and glue them to the inside of the box. See the illustration for location details.

7

Using a plug cutter, make the plugs to fill the countersunk holes. Don't drill completely through the wood blank. This saves you the trouble of having to remove each plug from the inside of the cutter.

8

Cut the plugs free from the wood blank using your band saw.

9

Put glue in the countersunk holes.

10

Install the plugs and gently tap them home.

11

While the glue is still wet, sand the plugs level with the side. Sanding while the glue is wet lets the sanding dust mix with the glue and fills in any slight gaps around the plugs.

12

The plugs are almost undetectable after sanding. If you want to spice things up a bit, make the plugs from a contrasting-color wood. This tells folks that you are unafraid to proclaim that you used screws to assemble your box.

13

After the box is assembled, cut the lid to size and cut shallow rabbets on each side, that is a small offset that will nestle into the box just a little. It's a built-in lid keeper.

14

You've seen this step before. Glue the ends to the bottom of the small box.

15

Glue the sides to complete the small box.

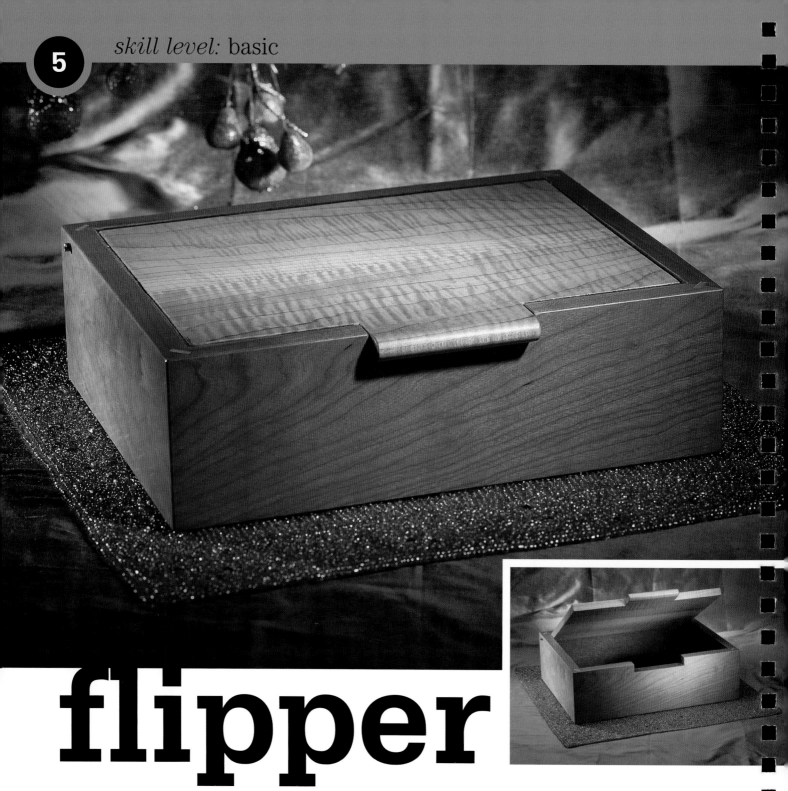

flipper

HERE'S A PROJECT THAT GIVES YOU INSIGHT into the world of keyed miter joints. (It's a world of mystery and intrigue.) How to clamp the miter joints is one of the little mysteries that will be revealed. You'll also get to do some fun cutting and shaping.

The hinging of the lid is different from the last project. It requires some accurate alignment of the lid and the box and a steady hand for drilling the pinhole. This is one of those times when access to a drill press is advantageous.

Several of the boxes in this book have flat lids that give you a chance to use some of that special wood you've been saving for just the right project. This project is no exception. I used some curly maple I've had for several years.

As to the function of the box — well, it's just a box. I lined it with felt so delicate items such as jewelry or pistons from small-engine blocks could be stored safely.

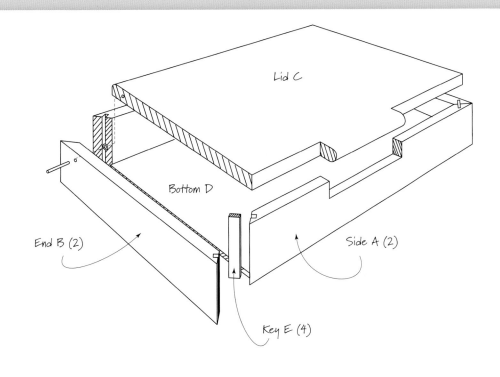

Lid C

Bottom D

End B (2)

Side A (2)

Key E (4)

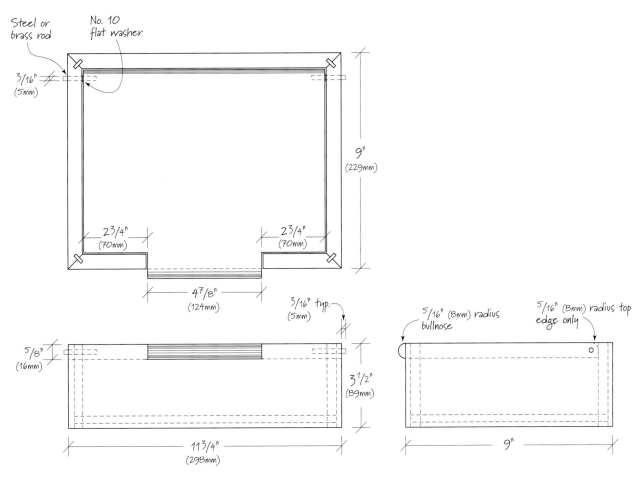

Steel or brass rod

No. 10 flat washer

3/16" (5mm)

9" (229mm)

2 3/4" (70mm)

2 3/4" (70mm)

4 7/8" (124mm)

3/16" typ. (5mm)

5/8" (16mm)

3 1/2" (89mm)

11 3/4" (298mm)

5/16" (8mm) radius bullnose

5/16" (8mm) radius top edge only

9"

inches (millimeters)

REFERENCE	QUANTITY	PART	STOCK	THICKNESS	(mm)	WIDTH	(mm)	LENGTH	(mm)
A	2	sides	cherry	5/8	(16)	3 1/2	(89)	11 3/4	(298)
B	2	ends	cherry	5/8	(16)	3 1/2	(89)	9	(229)
C	1	lid	curly maple	1/2	(13)	8 3/4	(222)	10 3/8	(264)
D	1	bottom	plywood	1/4	(6)	8 1/2	(216)	11 1/4	(286)
E	4	keys	maple	1/8	(3)	5/8	(16)	3 1/2	(89)

Tools needed

hand saw with miter box

60-, 100-, 120-, 150- and 220-grit sandpapers

sanding block (see sanding block sidebar, page 11)

block plane

random-orbit electric sander

power miter saw

table saw

Hardware & Supplies

2   steel or brass rods 3/16" diameter (5mm) x 1 3/8 (35mm)

2   #10 (5mm) steel or brass flat washers

Cut the parts to dimension as shown in the cutting list. Then cut the miters on both ends of the sides and ends. You can use a power miter saw, a miter box and handsaw or a table saw to cut the miters. (When cutting the miters, test-fit the cut using scraps. Put two of the mitered ends together and check that they form a perfectly square joint.) Tilt the table saw blade to a 45° miter and cut the slots for the keys. Position the slot toward the inside of the miter so it can be cut 5/16" (8mm) deep.

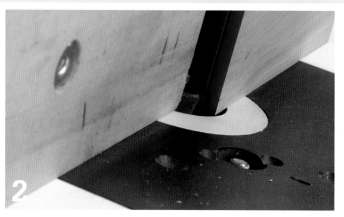

You can machine all kinds of profiles and slots into parts with mitered ends, and they'll all match up when you put the miter joints together. When you cut the rabbet for the bottom panel, cut it the total length of the side and end parts with no worries about the rabbet showing after the box is assembled.

Use a table saw to cut the opening for the lid in the front piece (side A in drawing). Draw the opening on the front and set the saw blade height to the depth of the opening. Use a miter gauge with a backer board attached to it to feed the part over the saw blade. Make two cuts to define the width of the opening and nibble away the rest of the cutout. Slide the part over the saw blade from side to side to clean up the cutout. This makes a perfectly square cutout that's ready to go to assembly.

When you cut the keys, cut them longer than needed. You can trim them after the glue dries. You could use eight bar clamps to make this assembly (which is a lot like performing the spinning-plates act) or you can use two band clamps as I've done here. The steel corner blocks along with the bands pull these miters together. And if you've cut your miters properly (which I know you have), the assembly squares itself quite nicely.

5

If you're like me, you don't trust yourself completely. I made doubly sure the assembly would be square by clamping a square block in the box until the glue dried.

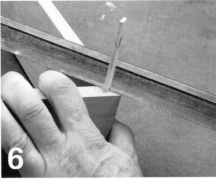

6

Use a small handsaw to trim the keys flush to the box. I'm not actually cutting into my finger. The angle of the camera makes it look that way but rest assured I've grown attached to my digits and I want to keep them.

7

Use the table saw to cut the large notches that make the handle on the lid.

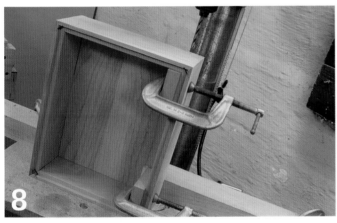

8

Drill the hinge-pin holes using a drill press. Drill this hole through the side and into the edge of the lid in one motion. This assures accuracy. I clamped spacer blocks inside the box and held the lid against them to keep the lid in the proper location.

9

Shape the edges of the handle using a block plane. Then sand the lid smooth.

10

After lining the box with felt, install the metal rods. I chucked the rods in my drill and drove them into the holes. I found this a good way to align the rod with the hole in the lid. Be sure to install the washer between the lid and the inside of the box. The washers hold the lid centered in the box and give the lid something to rub against when it's opened and closed.

11

Use a hammer to drive (gently please!) the rods home.

slider

THIS BOX IS PATTERNED after the candle boxes once made by the Shakers. You'll learn how to cut grooves and tenons and how to raise a panel. The critical part of this project is the fitting of the raised-panel lid. It should slide smoothly in the grooves.

The groove-and-tenon method of construction is a tried-and-tested method that

you can adapt to the making of drawers and cabinets. It ensures perfect alignment of all parts and great strength of the finished project.

Use this box to store candles and maybe a box of matches. When the lights go out, you'll have candlelight in a jiffy, provided you can find the box in the dark.

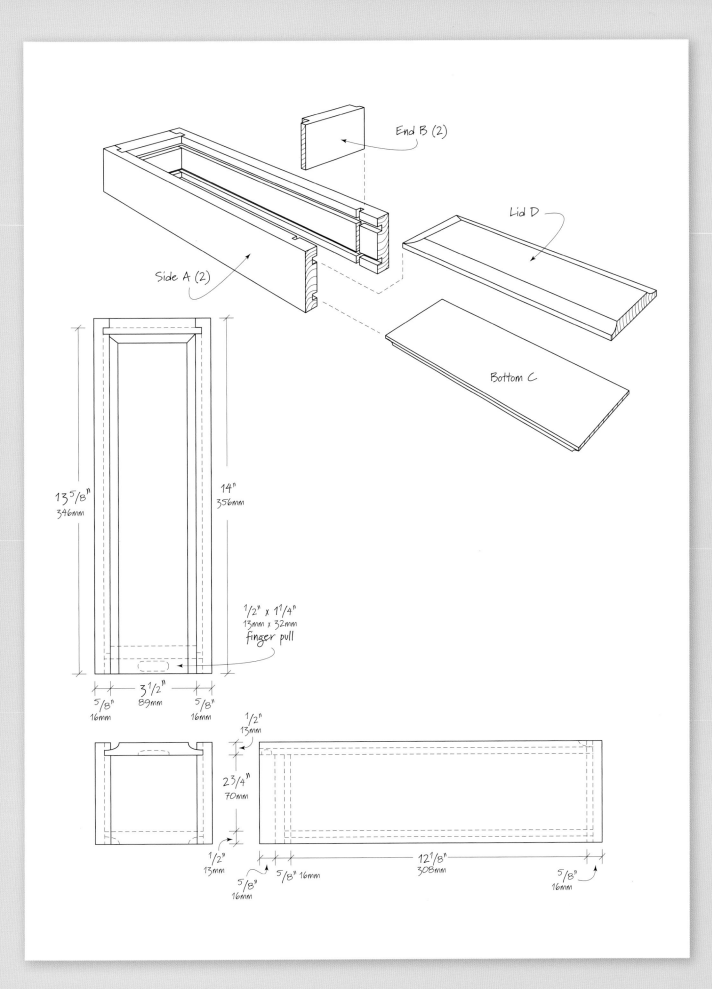

End B (2)

Lid D

Side A (2)

Bottom C

13 5/8"
346mm

14"
356mm

1/2" x 1 1/4"
13mm x 32mm
finger pull

3 1/2"
89mm

5/8"
16mm

5/8"
16mm

1/2"
13mm

2 3/4"
70mm

1/2"
13mm

5/8"
16mm

5/8" 16mm

12 1/8"
308mm

5/8"
16mm

inches (millimeters)

REFERENCE	QUANTITY	PART	STOCK	THICKNESS	(mm)	WIDTH	(mm)	LENGTH	(mm)
A	2	sides	english oak	$5/8$	(16)	4	(102)	14	(356)
B	2	ends	english oak	$5/8$	(16)	4	(102)	4	(102)
C	1	bottom	english oak	$1/2$	(13)	$3^7/8$	(98)	$12^5/8$	(321)
D	1	lid	english oak	$1/2$	(13)	$3^{13}/16$	(97)	$13^5/8$	(346)

Hardware & Supplies

spray or wipe-on lacquer

Tools needed

handsaw with miter box

60-, 100-, 120-, 150- and 220-grit sandpapers

No. 0000 steel wool

sanding block (see sanding block sidebar page 11)

block plane

table saw

combination square

bench plane

random-orbit electric sander

stationary sander (optional)

Lay the sides with their top edges touching. Draw the locations of the grooves for the two ends, the bottom and the lid.

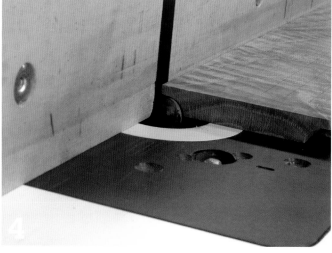

Cut the grooves on the table saw using a dado blade. You can also use a router table with a straight bit in the router.

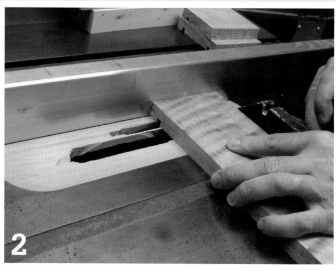

Cut the tenons on the ends. To set the saw for the proper blade height, use scrap wood planed to the same thickness as the ends to make samples.

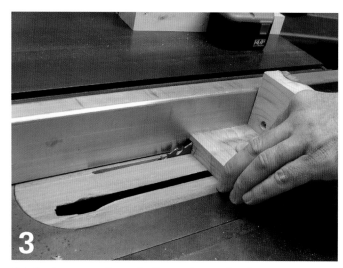

I used a core box router bit to shape the raised-panel bottom and lid parts.

By moving the router table fence back about ⅛" (3mm), I made another cut on the raised panels to get the proper length for the edges of the raised panels.

Use the same core box bit to cut the finger pull in the bottom front edge of the lid. Use a miter gauge to help hold the panel steady when making the plunge cut. The depth of the finger pull is about ³⁄₁₆" (5mm).

7

Apply glue to the tenons and grooves and assemble the box. Don't glue the bottom panel. It needs to move with seasonal changes in humidity.

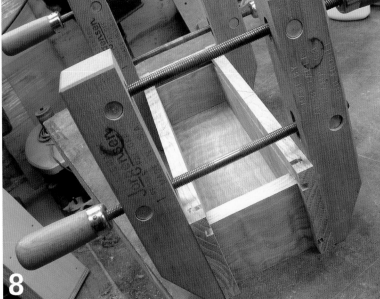

8

Use wooden hand screws to clamp the box together. The clamps shown are great for clamping a small project like this because they put even pressure along the entire length of the joints. When the glue is dry, insert the lid. If the lid is too snug or doesn't slide easily, fit it by sanding or planing the bottom of the lid until the tenons on the edges are the proper thickness to slide smoothly in the grooves. After the finish has been applied, it should slide even more smoothly. Apply some wax in the grooves for the ultimate in lid-sliding smoothness! If you're fitting the lid in winter, allow a little extra clearance in the grooves. The lid will expand in the summer and could bind if you haven't allowed for it.

ALL YOU NEED TO BUILD
THIS BOX is a 10' (3m) piece
of crown moulding and some
sugar pine, which is sometimes
called select pine. This project
was an exercise that involved
making a box using crown
moulding in a manner that is
not usually associated with this
type of moulding.

Except for the carving, this
project goes together quickly.
The possibilities of cutting and
combining the moulding are
many. I toyed with several ideas
before I settled on this box design. For example, I could have

used a ripped section of the
moulding laid flat to frame the
panel or a recessed base instead
of feet.

This project teaches you
how to make an interlocking
lap joint that holds the dividers together. You'll also make a
raised panel for the lid. Carving
the lid is optional, but I suggest
you give it a try. The sugar pine
used to make the panel is perfect for carving.

Use this box to store your
collection of rocks, thimbles,
marbles, seashells or other tiny
keepsakes.

crowning touch

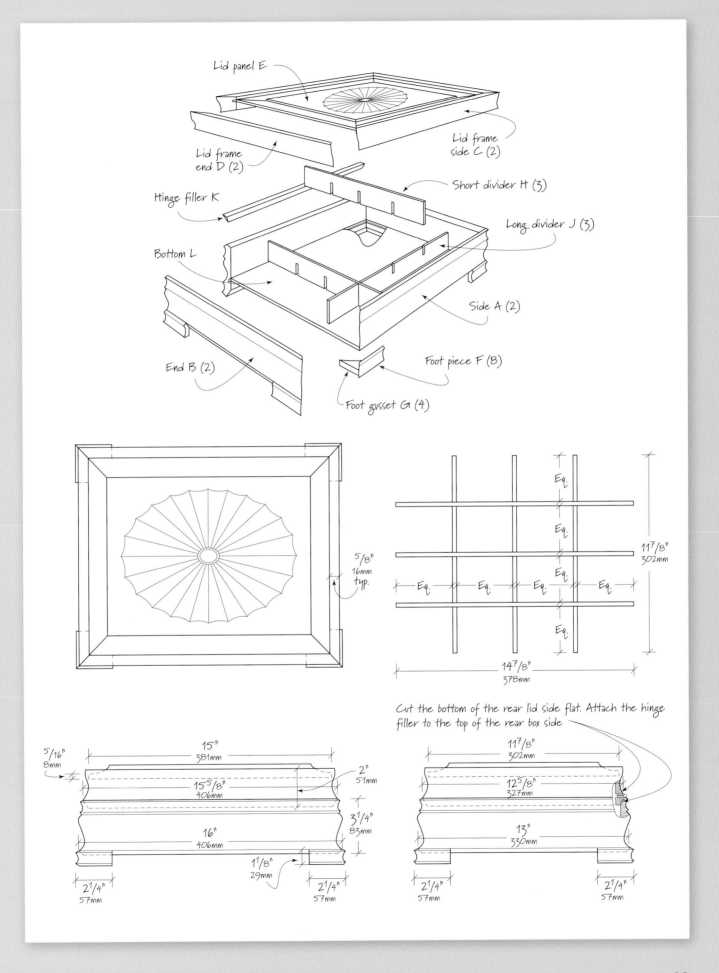

Lid panel E

Lid frame side C (2)

Lid frame end D (2)

Hinge filler K

Short divider H (3)

Long divider J (3)

Bottom L

Side A (2)

End B (2)

Foot piece F (8)

Foot gusset G (4)

5/8"
16mm
typ.

Eq.

Eq.

Eq.

Eq.

Eq.

Eq.

Eq.

Eq.

Eq.

11⁷/₈"
302mm

14⁷/₈"
378mm

Cut the bottom of the rear lid side flat. Attach the hinge filler to the top of the rear box side

5/16"
8mm

15"
381mm

2"
51mm

15⁵/₈"
406mm

3¹/₄"
83mm

16"
406mm

1¹/₈"
29mm

2¹/₄"
57mm

2¹/₄"
57mm

11⁷/₈"
302mm

12⁵/₈"
327mm

13"
330mm

2¹/₄"
57mm

2¹/₄"
57mm

inches (millimeters)

REFERENCE	QUANTITY	PART	STOCK	THICKNESS	(mm)	WIDTH	(mm)	LENGTH	(mm)
A	2	sides	pine	⅝	(16)	3¼	(83)	16	(406)
B	2	ends	pine	⅝	(16)	3¼	(83)	13	(330)
C	2	lid frame sides	pine	⅝	(16)	2	(51)	12⅝	(321)
D	2	lid frame ends	pine	⅝	(16)	2	(51)	15⅝	(397)
E	1	lid panel	sugar pine	⅝	(16)	11¾	(298)	14⅞	(378)
F	8	foot pieces	pine	⅝	(16)	1⅛	(29)	2¼	(57)
G	4	foot gussets	plywood	½	(13)	1½	(38)	1½	(38)
H	2	dividers	pine	¼	(6)	2	(51)	11⅞	(302)
J	2	dividers	pine	¼	(6)	2	(51)	14⅞	(378)
K	1	hinge filler	pine	½	(13)	½	(13)	15½	(394)
L	1	bottom	plywood	¼	(6)	12¼	(311)	15¼	(387)

Tools needed

handsaw with miter box

60-, 100-, 120-, 150- and 220-grit sandpapers

No. 0000 steel wool

sanding block (see sanding block sidebar page 11)

block plane

bench plane

random-orbit electric sander

stationary sander (optional)

Hardware & Supplies

1 pair	1¼" x 2" (32mm x 51mm) brass hinges
spray or wipe-on lacquer	

Cut the crown moulding to length with 45° miters on both ends. Cut the miters using a miter saw, with the moulding either laying flat on the saw's bed and tilting the saw blade to cut a 45° bevel or standing the moulding up against the saw's fence and setting the saw to cut a 45° miter. Cut a groove in the moulding for the bottom panel using either the table saw or a router table set up with a straight bit.

Cut the pieces for the feet by ripping the cove-shaped section from the crown moulding. Cut the foot pieces to length. Then cut a 45° miter on one end of each piece. Remember to cut left and right pieces (four of each).

Glue the miters together using a left and right piece for each foot. Cut the gussets in a triangle shape, curve the long side of the gusset as shown in the photo and glue them to the foot assemblies. (Why cut the curve you ask? It helps hide the gusset after the box is assembled and on its feet.) Then glue the foot assemblies to the bottom of the box.

4

For the lid frame parts, use the leftovers from the foot pieces you ripped. This is a no-waste project! Cut the groove for the lid panel using either the table saw or the router table.

5

The select (sugar) pine that I found at my local home improvement center was 4" (102mm) wide, so I needed to glue up several pieces to get the proper width for the lid panel. I then used a panel-raising bit in the router table to cut the profile on the lid panel.

6

In order for the lid to open properly, cut a full-length notch in the back rail of the lid. Cut the notch on the table saw. Make it in two cuts — just like cutting a rabbet. This creates a square edge for the hinges. Then cut the mortise for the hinge. I like to cut the full-depth mortise in the box. Then it's only a matter of mounting the hinge directly to the lid.

HINGE FILLER

7

Cut the hinge filler and glue it to the top inside edge of the back side of the box. The filler is triangular in shape and both ends have miters cut to match the top-edge angle of the end pieces. The box inspector showed up unexpectedly and wanted to take a closer look at my work. I complied and all was found to be in order. If only I could teach Izzy to do some sanding!

8

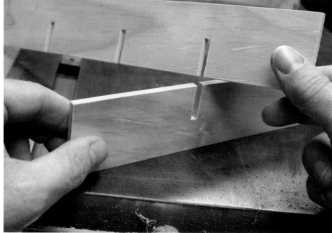

Here's how to make the locking lap joints. Set up a dado cutter that cuts a slot whose width is the same dimension as the thickness of the divider parts. (If you don't have a dado cutter, set up a straight bit in your router table. When you mill the divider parts, be sure they are the same thickness as the diameter of the router bit.) Make one slot cut in the center of the parts. Then register the two other slot cuts using the table saw's fence. Make the first cut and flip the parts end for end and make the second cut. You can make the cuts in each set of three divider parts at the same time. Mark the parts using a triangle — if there is a slight variance in the centering the center slot (perish the thought!), you will still be able to assemble the dividers, and they'll line up properly.

9

This is a trick I use when carving the top and bottom plates for the arch-top guitars I make — drill a series of 1/8"-diameter (3mm) holes about 3/16" (5mm) deep in what will be the lowest carved part of the scroll. When the hole disappears as you're carving, you've reached the proper depth. This will ensure consistent depth in the carving and that you won't accidentally carve through the top!

10

I defined the outside of the scroll and the inside ellipse using a V-groove knife, then I carved the scroll using an 1/8"-wide (3mm) and a 1/2"-wide (13mm) gouge. I chose to leave the tooling marks.

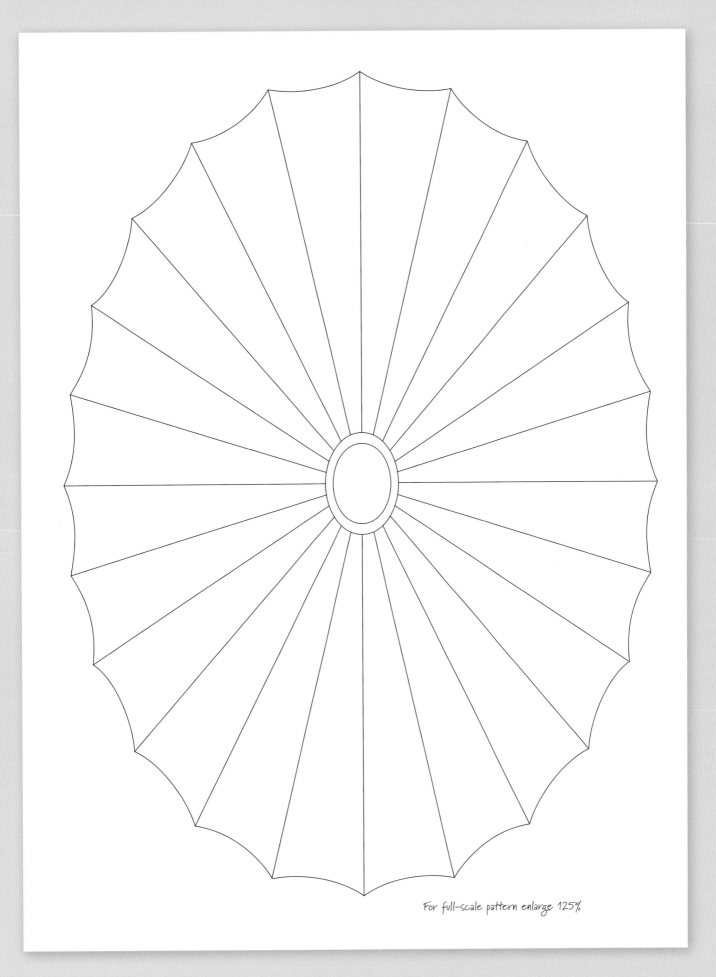

For full-scale pattern enlarge 125%.

THIS BOX IS SPECIFICALLY MADE TO HOLD LETTERS. You remember those, don't you? When you receive a letter and hold it in your hands, you have the actual paper that the writer held in his or her hands and you have their writing right there in front of you. It's personal — and that's what letters are supposed to be. Saving e-mails or phone messages just isn't the same.

This project will teach you how to make a solid-wood frame-and-panel lid using mortise-and-tenon joinery and how to cut finger joints using the table saw. This lid also has built-in handles that are cradled in the sides of the box.

One of the great things about building boxes is that you need only small amounts of wood. I had one 4'-long (1.2m) board of teak that I've had in my wood racks for almost 20 years! This was the project that I was waiting for so I could use that wood. With a small scrap of cherry for the lid's panel and some red oak for the dividers, I was good to go.

why don't
you write?

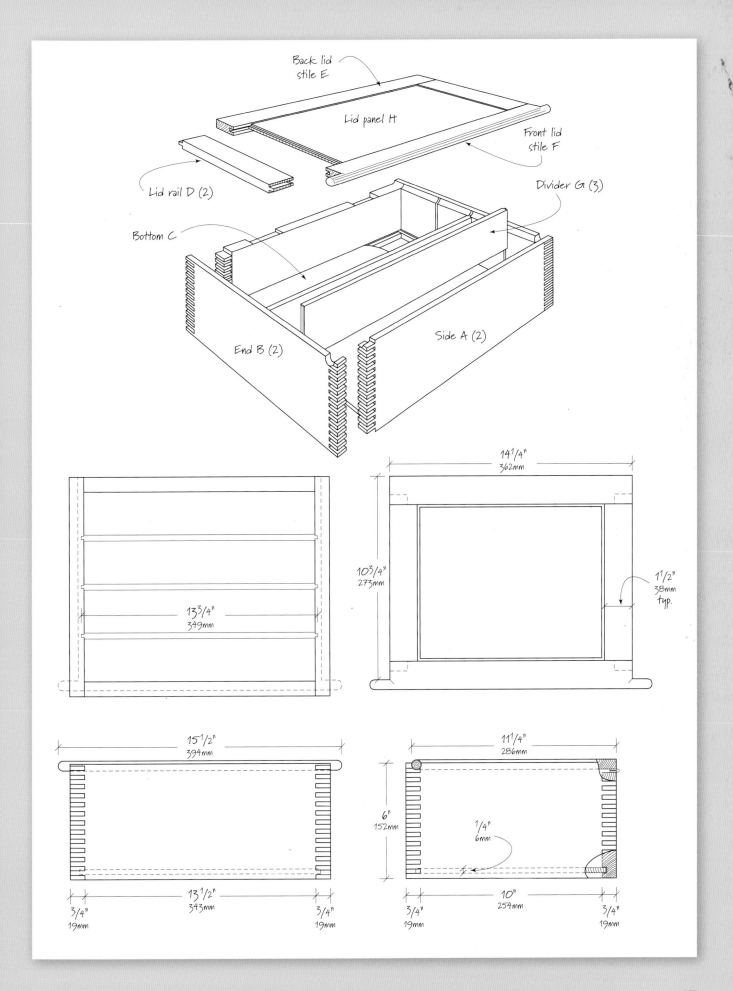

Back lid
stile E

Lid panel H

Front lid
stile F

Lid rail D (2)

Divider G (3)

Bottom C

End B (2)

Side A (2)

14¹/4"
362mm

10³/4"
273mm

1¹/2"
38mm
typ.

13³/4"
349mm

15¹/2"
394mm

6"
152mm

¹/4"
6mm

13¹/2"
343mm

3/4"
19mm

3/4"
19mm

11¹/4"
286mm

10"
254mm

3/4"
19mm

3/4"
19mm

inches (millimeters)

REFERENCE	QUANTITY	PART	STOCK	THICKNESS	(mm)	WIDTH	(mm)	LENGTH	(mm)
A	2	sides	teak	3/4	(19)	6	(152)	15	(381)
B	2	ends	teak	3/4	(19)	6	(152)	11 1/2	(292)
C	1	bottom	plywood	1/4	(6)	10 1/2	(267)	14	(356)
D	2	lid rails	teak	1/2	(13)	1 1/2	(38)	8 3/4	(222)
E	1	back lid stile	teak	1/2	(13)	1 1/2	(38)	13 1/4	(337)
F	1	front lid stile	teak	1/2	(13)	1 1/2	(38)	15 1/2	(394)
G	3	dividers	red oak	1/4	(6)	3 1/2	(89)	14 1/4	(362)
H	1	lid panel	cherry	1/2	(13)	8 5/8	(219)	12 1/4	(311)

Tools needed

hand saw with miter box

table saw

60-, 100-, 120-, 150- and 220-grit sandpapers

No. 0000 steel wool

sanding block (see sanding block sidebar page 11)

block plane

bench plane

random-orbit electric sander

stationary sander (optional)

Hardware & Supplies

1 pr.	1" x 1 1/2" (25mm x 38mm) butt hinges
	spray or rub-on lacquer

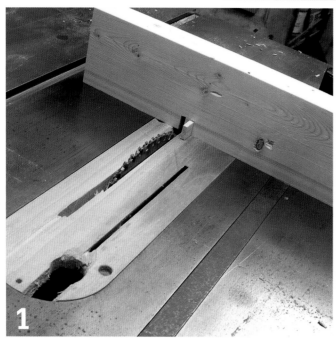

Install a 1/4"-wide (6mm) dado cutter in the table saw or a 1/4"-diameter (6mm) router bit in your router table. Mount a fence to your miter gauge. Cut a slot in the fence and fit a piece of wood the exact width of the slot into the slot. This is the finger-joint key. Remove the fence and move it one slot width to the right of the key, then reattach the fence to the miter gauge. This is your finger-joint cutting fixture.

Mark the top edges of all the drawer's end and side parts. Keep these top edges oriented to your left when you are cutting slots. This will ensure that all the parts line up when you finish cutting the finger-joint slots. Start by holding a box end part against the key and cut a slot. I suggest that you use some scrap wood and practice cutting slots and matching the ends to be sure you clearly understand this procedure.

3

Slide this slot over the key and cut a second slot. Continue moving the box end over and cutting slots. Remember to keep the marked edges of the parts to your left as you flip the parts to cut slots in both ends.

4

After you've cut the slots in both ends of the box's end parts, turn the end part around so the top edge is to your right. Slide the key into the top slot. Then hold one of the box's side parts against the end part. (You should have the top edges of both parts together.) Then cut a slot in the edge of the side part. (This slot is flush with the edge of the side part.)

5

Continue cutting slots as before. Do this for both side parts.

6

The end and side parts should match!

7

To cut the grooves for the bottom, set up your table with a ¼"-diameter (6mm) straight bit. Make stopped grooves in the end and side parts. See the illustration for details. Note the pencil lines on the router fence. These show me where to hold the end of the part when I start the cut and where to stop the cut. To start the cut, hold the end of the part above the turning router bit and slowly drop it on the bit. This is called a plunge cut. Run the part along the fence until you get to the end of the cut.

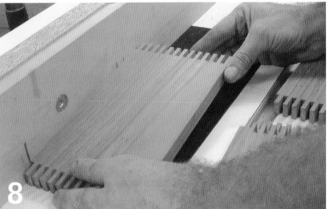

8

When you reach the end of the cut, stop and carefully lift the part off the router bit. If you feel uncomfortable doing this while the router bit is turning, turn off the router before lifting.

Cut the slots for the dividers using an ⅛"-diameter (3mm) router bit. Set the router fence to cut the middle slot in the center of the box's sides. Be sure to set the fence parallel to the miter-gauge slot in the tabletop. Then use a miter gauge with a fence to feed the part over the router bit. After making these cuts, set the fence to cut the other two slots. Cut one slot, then turn the part end for end and make the other cut. This ensures the slots are an equal distance from both ends of the parts.

Cut out the lid frame parts. Then make the groove for the tenons and lid panel. Set your table saw's fence to make the first cut slightly off center. Turn the part end for end and make another cut. This will ensure the groove is centered in the part.

Cut the tenons by setting the saw's fence to cut the length the same as the depth of the groove you cut in step 10. (Normally tenons are cut slightly shorter than the depth of the groove or mortise. The resulting gap at the bottom of the groove will allow for glue. These tenons and grooves will show on the lid. It's much neater to seat the tenon firmly at the bottom of the groove.) When setting the fence, measure to the side of the blade farthest from the fence. Then set the blade height to about one-third the thickness of the rails. You may need to raise or lower the blade until you get the correct tenon thickness. Then cut the tenons on the rails.

Cut the lid's panel to size. (Note that in the cutting list, the panel is cut slightly narrower than the math would tell you. This is to allow for the seasonal movement of the panel in the frame.) Then cut the rabbets in the edges of the panel. I used a dado cutter and the router table. You can cut these rabbets on the table saw, but then you'll need to sand away the saw blade marks. This style of router bit is made to cut cleanly and no sanding cleanup is necessary.

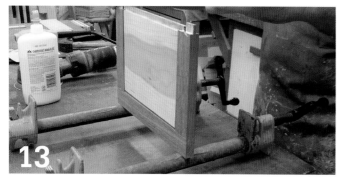

Cut notches to create the handles in the ends of the front rail. Test-fit all the lid's parts before applying any glue. If you need to make an adjustment, you can still do it. When all fits properly, apply glue to the faces of the tenons and assemble the frame. Do not apply glue to the panel. It needs to be free to make seasonal movements.

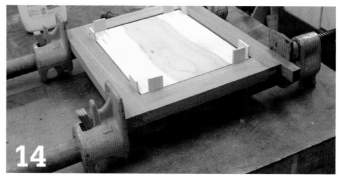

The reveal around the edges of the panel in relation to the frame is about ⅛" (3mm). Cut some spacers to this thickness and put them between the panel and the frame, so the panel is centered in the frame.

15

On the inside of the lid, install a small nail through the frame and into the center of each end of the panel. Be sure the nail doesn't go through the face of the lid! These nails will hold the panel in place and allow it to expand and contract equally from the center of the frame. Cut the nail flush to the frame.

16

Cut the half-circle slots for the lid handles in the sides of the box using a rat-tail or round file.

17

Round over the edges of the lid using a spokeshave or block plane. Then, using a wood rasp and some files, shape the handles on the front of the lid to fit into the half-circle slots in the sides of the box. Sand the roundovers smooth.

18

After marking the locations for the hinges, use each hinge as a template and score around it using a razor knife.

19

Cut the mortises for the hinges using a chisel. These mortises are cut to accept the full thickness of the hinge. That way, you don't need to cut a matching mortise in the lid. I do this on about 90 percent of the butt hinges I install. It makes the job go quicker, and they look great. If you want to cut two matching mortises, their depths will be only half the thickness of the hinge. There's not a lot of difference in the look of the hinge orientation in relation to the lid when it's installed. (See illustration at right.) It's up to you.

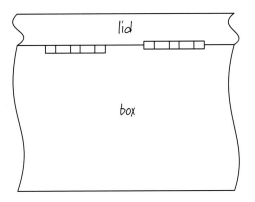

safely kept

ABOUT 300 YEARS AGO, when I was a Cub Scout, there was a project article in *Boy's Life* magazine that showed how to make a wooden safe with real moving tumblers. I made that project and was always proud that no one could open it if they didn't know the combina-tion. I had that safe for years. This is a smaller version of that project.

This project shows you how to glue mitered joints and gives you a chance to experiment with a textured painted finish. Careful measuring and fitting are necessities. The combination lock will work as promised, but only if you exercise patience in fitting all the parts together!

I like the idea that all the parts are made of wood (or at least wood by-products) and that they work smoothly to-gether.

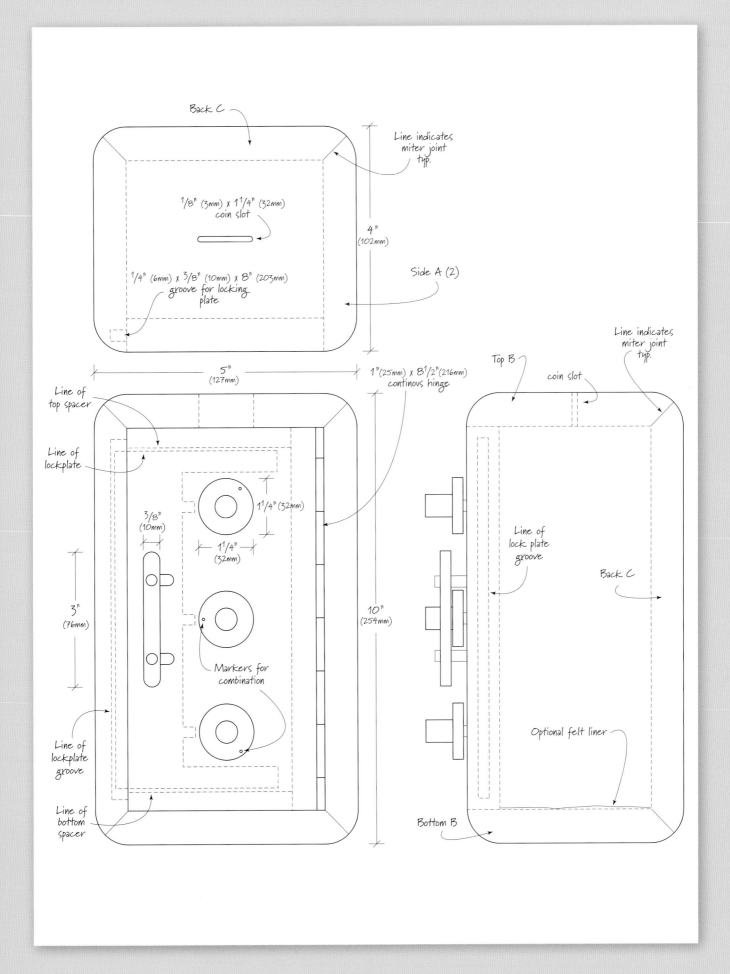

Back C

Line indicates miter joint typ.

1/8" (3mm) x 1 1/4" (32mm) coin slot

4" (102mm)

1/4" (6mm) x 3/8" (10mm) x 8" (203mm) groove for locking plate

Side A (2)

5" (127mm)

1"(25mm) x 8 1/2"(216mm) continous hinge

Line indicates miter joint typ.

Top B

coin slot

Line of top spacer

Line of lockplate

3/8" (10mm)

1 1/4" (32mm)

1 1/4" (32mm)

3" (76mm)

10" (254mm)

Line of lock plate groove

Back C

Markers for combination

Line of lockplate groove

Line of bottom spacer

Optional felt liner

Bottom B

inches (millimeters)

REFERENCE	QUANTITY	PART	STOCK	THICKNESS	(mm)	WIDTH	(mm)	LENGTH	(mm)
A	2	sides	MDF	$3/4$	(19)	5	(127)	10	(254)
B	2	top/bottom	MDF	$3/4$	(19)	5	(127)	6	(152)
C	1	back	MDF	$3/4$	(19)	6	(152)	10	254
D	1	door		$3/4$	(19)	$4^{1/4}$	(108)	$8^{1/2}$	(216)
E	2	front/back	hardboard	$1/4$	(6)	$4^{1/4}$	(108)	$8^{1/2}$	(216)
F	2	top/bottom spacers	hardboard	$1/4$	(6)	$1/2$	(13)	$3^{3/4}$	(95)
G	1	side spacer	hardboard	$1/4$	(6)	$1/2$	(13)	$8^{1/2}$	(216)
H	1	lock plate	hardboard	$1/4$	(6)	$3^{11/16}$	(94)	$7^{7/16}$	(189)
I	3	inner tumblers	hardboard	$1/4$	(6)	$1^{1/4}$ dia.	(32)		
J	3	outer tumblers	hardboard	$1/4$	(6)	$1^{1/4}$ dia.	(32)		
K	3	tumbler dowels	hardwood	$1/4$ dia.	(6)			$13/16$	(21)
L	3	tumbler knobs	hardwood	$1/2$ dia.	(13)			$5/8$	(16)
M	1	handle	hardwood	$1/4$	(6)	$1/2$	(13)	3	(76)
N	2	handle dowels	hardwood	$1/4$ dia.	(6)			$1^{3/16}$	(30)

Tools needed

drill ("egg beater" style or handheld electric)

$3/16$" (5mm) and $1/8$" (3mm) twist drills

drill countersink

Phillips screwdriver

60-, 100-, 120-, 150- and 220-grit sandpapers

sanding block (see sanding block sidebar page 11)

block plane

random-orbit electric sander

router mounted in router table

table saw

Hardware & Supplies

1		1" x $8^{1/2}$" (25mm x 216mm) continuous hinge (brass or black)
1 can		hammered-texture spray paint
1 pint		gloss lacquer top coat
1 pc.		$3^{1/2}$" x $4^{1/2}$" (89mm x 114) felt cloth liner for inside bottom of bank (optional)

Back C
Top/bottom (2)
Side A (2)
Side spacer
Top & bottom spacers
Back
Inner tumbler (3)
Outer tumbler (3)
Tumbler dowel (3)
Tumbler knob (3)
Lock plate
Front
Handle dowel (2)
Handle

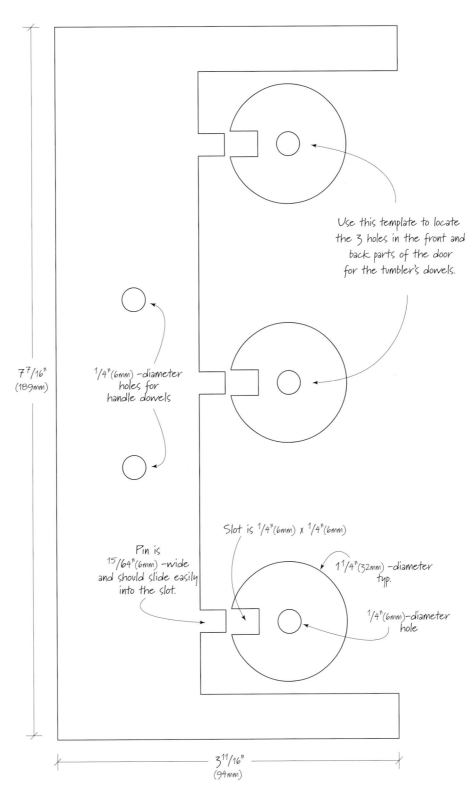

$7\frac{7}{16}"$
(189mm)

Use this template to locate the 3 holes in the front and back parts of the door for the tumbler's dowels.

$\frac{1}{4}"$(6mm) –diameter holes for handle dowels

Slot is $\frac{1}{4}"$(6mm) x $\frac{1}{4}"$(6mm)

Pin is $\frac{15}{64}"$(6mm) –wide and should slide easily into the slot.

$1\frac{1}{4}"$(32mm) –diameter typ.

$\frac{1}{4}"$(6mm)–diameter hole

$3\frac{11}{16}"$
(94mm)

Copy this pattern at 100% to use as a template.

After cutting the box parts to size, you can use a bevel-cutting router bit to cut the 45° bevel on the parts. Do this operation in two or three steps. Cutting it all once could cause your router to internally hemorrhage, the bit to burn or the part to be pulled out of your hands. None of these is a good thing.

Use a miter gauge to guide the narrow parts past the router bit. As you can see, all is calm and peaceful because this final cut is a light pass. Be sure to use good dust collection when cutting MDF. The dust is nasty stuff.

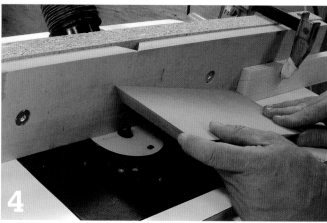

By taking your time, the cuts will be clean and ready to go. You can also make these cuts on the table saw. It's your choice. Why did I use the router? I have good dust collection on my router table and not on my table saw.

Cut the groove for the locking plate now. If you wait until after you've assembled the box, you'll have a real challenge cutting this groove.

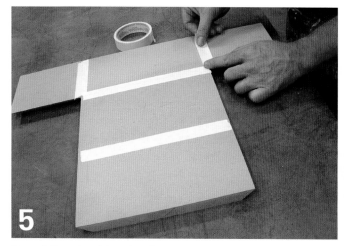

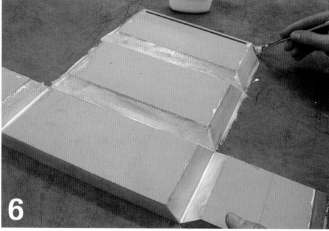

I taped the miter joints for glue up.

Flip the taped parts and add glue to the miter joints. MDF's end grain is like a blotter. The glue almost immediately soaks into the wood. Apply the glue liberally.

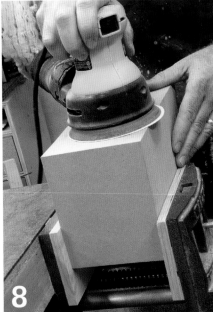

Sand the box smooth so the joints are clean and sharp. Remember to wear a dust mask. The sander has a bag and it does a great job of collecting the dust but there are always some stray particles eager to jump into your lungs.

7 This is the fun part — folding the box. It always amazes me that you have all these parts laying flat and gluey and the next thing you know you're taping the open joint and walking away while the glue dries. A box is born.

9 I used a ⅛" (3mm) straight router bit to cut the slot in the top of the box. Do this in several passes. Note the start and stop blocks clamped to the router table fence. This makes it easy to cut this slot accurately. Measure your location twice so you're sure the slot is centered.

10 Set up a ⅜" (10mm) roundover router bit and round all the outside corners. That's it. The box is ready for sanding.

11 Now comes the fun part. (Well, at least I thought it was fun.) Use a hole saw to cut out the tumblers. You're doing two things at the same time here — you're cutting the discs and drilling the ¼" (6mm) hole (perfectly centered) for the dowels. Don't feed the drill too fast or it will burn the wood. Easy does it.

12 You'll have to cut a notch in the inside tumblers. Set up a V-jig to hold the tumbler steady while you drill a hole in the edge of the disc.

Use a file to square the slots in the tumblers.

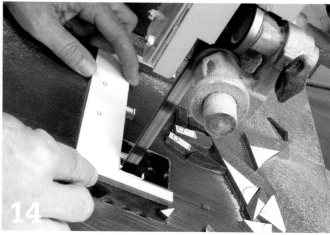

I recommend making a copy of the full-size pattern for the locking plate. Attach it to the hardboard with a spray adhesive. Now you can cut it on the lines.

Use the pattern to locate the holes for the tumbler's dowels and the slots for the handle. This is what all the parts look like when ready for assembly. It helps to lay them out so you can see what goes where.

Glue the spacers to the inside back of the door. Use the locking plate as a template for locating these spacers. You want the locking plate to smoothly slide between the top and bottom spacers. Take your time and get this right. That way, you only have to do it once.

Glue the inside tumblers to the tumbler dowels. The dowels go through the tumblers and into the holes in the back of the door. Let the glue dry before moving on. When the glue is dry, clean up any excess glue that may have run through the holes. You want these tumblers to turn freely. Test them in the back holes.

Leave the tumblers in the back holes and put the front plate in place. Check the fit and turning ability of the tumblers. If any of them bind, lightly sand the dowels until the tumblers turn smoothly and freely.

Glue the door front to the back only at the spacers. Test the tumblers to be sure they still turn freely. Adjust the front plate until they do. When the glue dries, that's all she wrote.

The tumbler plates are the same thickness as the spacer. I added thin cardboard shims so the tumblers would turn freely. You could, as an option, sand the tumblers so they are a little thinner than the spacers.

Glue the knobs to the outside tumblers before gluing them to the door. These little guys are now waiting to be attached to the tumbler dowels that stick out the door front.

Cut out the parts for the sliding handle and glue them together. I wanted the dowels on the handle to protrude slightly from the front of the handle, so I placed a piece of scrap hardboard underneath for a spacer. I let the handle sit like this until the glue dried. Then I cut away the dried glue with a razor knife.

Glue the tumbler handles to the tumbler dowels. Install the locking plate by sliding it into the door, then put the sliding handle dowels through the slots in the door front and make sure they fit into the holes in the locking plate. I had to do a little fitting to get the handle to slide freely into the slots. Attach the hinge to the door, then attach it to the box. The handle will slide the locking plate back and forth, locking into the slots on the tumblers (when the slots are lined up) and sliding into the slot in the side of the box. This may take a little tuning up to get it all working correctly but it really does work! After you've finished the safe, decide what you want the combination to be. With the door open so the fingers on the locking plate are in the slots on the tumblers, paint little dots at the locations you choose for the combination. Then, when you close the door and turn the tumblers, no one will be able to crack your safe.

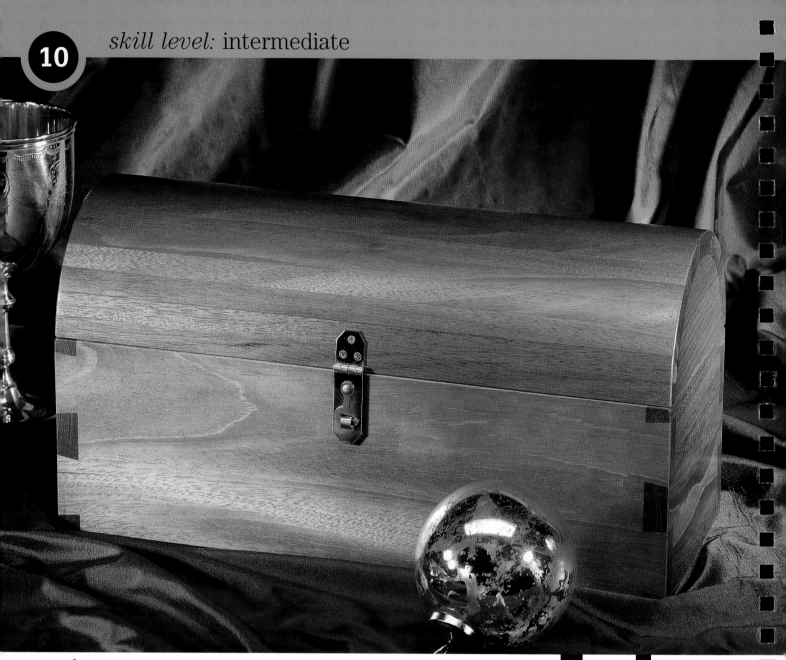

treasure this

I ALWAYS WANTED A BOX LIKE THIS when I was growing up. I had lots of treasures I needed to keep safe. If desired, you could also install a mortised lock to keep the contents of your box free from curious eyes and hands.

The techniques involved in making this box include cutting through-dovetails and making beveled slats using a router table. Neither of these techniques is difficult. The setups are straightforward and, with some practice, easy to do.

Making the coopered lid is also a matter of following a few basic steps. Coopering is a centuries-old method of making round stuff out of square stuff.

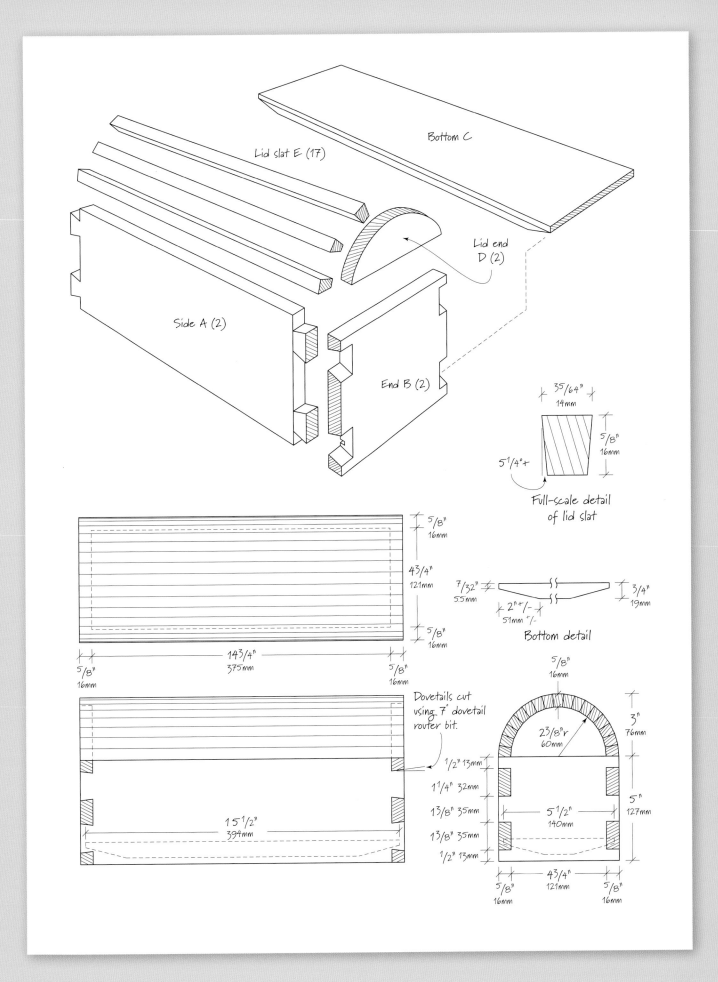

Bottom C

Lid slat E (17)

Lid end D (2)

Side A (2)

End B (2)

35/64"
14mm

5/8"
16mm

5 1/4°+

Full-scale detail
of lid slat

5/8"
16mm

4 3/4"
121mm

5/8"
16mm

14 3/4"
375mm

5/8"
16mm

5/8"
16mm

7/32"
5.5mm

2"+/-
51mm +/-

3/4"
19mm

Bottom detail

Dovetails cut
using 7° dovetail
router bit.

15 1/2"
394mm

1/2" 13mm

1 1/4" 32mm

1 3/8" 35mm

1 3/8" 35mm

1/2" 13mm

5/8"
16mm

2 3/8"r
60mm

3"
76mm

5 1/2"
140mm

5"
127mm

4 3/4"
121mm

5/8"
16mm

5/8"
16mm

inches (millimeters)

REFERENCE	QUANTITY	PART	STOCK	THICKNESS	(mm)	WIDTH	(mm)	LENGTH	(mm)
A	2	sides	mahogany	⁵⁄₈	(16)	6	(152)	16	(406)
B	2	ends	mahogany	⁵⁄₈	(16)	5	(127)	6	(152)
C	1	bottom	pine	³⁄₄	(19)	5¹⁄₂	(140)	15¹⁄₂	(394)
D	2	lid ends	mahogany	⁵⁄₈	(16)	2³⁄₈	(60)	4³⁄₄	(121)
E	17	lid slats	mahogany	⁵⁄₈	(16)	⁹⁄₁₆	(14)	16	(406)

Hardware & Supplies

1	1" x 14³⁄₄" (25mm x 375mm) continuous hinge
8	No. 6 - ³⁄₄" (19mm) wood screws
12	6d finish nails
	spray or rub-on lacquer finish

Tools needed

drill ("egg beater" style or handheld electric)

³⁄₃₂" (2mm) twist drill

Phillips screwdriver

60-, 100-, 120-, 150- and 220-grit sandpapers

No. 0000 steel wool

sanding block (see sanding block sidebar page 11)

block plane or bench plane

random-orbit electric sander

table saw

band saw, jigsaw or coping saw

router table

dovetail router bit

straight router bit

1

If you can find boards wide enough to make this project, go for it. I had to glue up narrower boards to get the proper width.

2

When you've got the sides and ends cut to size, mark them using a triangle. When you're machining the parts, these marks will tell you which edge is up and which part is right or left or top or bottom.

YOU DECIDE You can use either the table saw or the router table to cut through-dovetail joints. See the sidebar "Cutting Dovetails Using the Table Saw". I suggest you read the sidebar before proceeding with this router-table operation. The sidebar will give you more detailed instructions about how the table-saw method works. Then you can choose the one you would like to use.

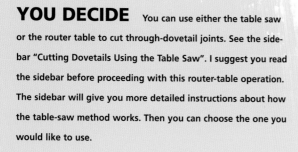

3

Set up a straight bit in your router table so the height of the bit is the same as the thickness of the box parts. Set the router table's fence parallel to the miter gauge slot in the tabletop. Set the miter gauge to 7°. This degree measurement is based on the 7° dovetail router bit you'll use to cut the tails.

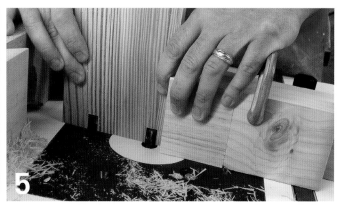

Determine what the spacing will be on your dovetails. I thought that one pin at each edge and one large pin in the middle looked good. Attach a stop block on the miter gauge fence and make the first cut. Keep the same edge of each part against the stop block. (Use the triangle marks to keep the parts oriented.) When you make the cuts in the other end of these parts, flip the parts end for end and keep the same edge against the block.

Put a spacer block against the stop block and make the second cut. Now set up the miter gauge fence so the 7° angle is opposite what you just cut. Then finish cutting the spaces to create the pins.

Install the dovetail router bit and set the miter gauge so it's square to the router table's fence

Mark the location of the pins on the side parts, using the end parts as a template. Cut the dovetails holding the parts securely against the miter gauge fence. I found that doing this freehand, rather than using a stop block, ensured better accuracy.

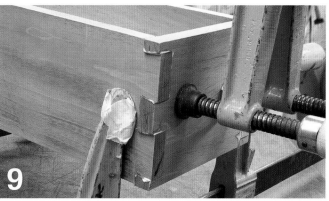

Use a bench plane to cut the bevels on the bottom panel. Furniture makers in the 18th and 19th centuries commonly used panels for bottoms. If it was good enough for them, it's good enough for this project! Plus, it gives you some practice using a hand plane.

Cut the groove for the bottom. Then glue the box together, capturing the bottom in the box. Don't use any glue to hold the bottom in place. It will be happy just sitting loose in the box.

10

Configure the grain of the wood vertically for the end parts. This will allow the wood to move seasonally with the top slats.

11

The method you'll use to make the top of the lid is called coopering. (It's used to make buckets, pails and barrels.) The slats for the lid need to be beveled on opposite edges. The bevel in this case is $5\frac{1}{4}+°$ [$(180° \div 17) \div 2 = 5\frac{1}{4}+°$]. Cut a strip of wood on your table saw to this bevel. Then attach the strip to a base and put it on your router table against the fence. Feed the slats past a straight bit.

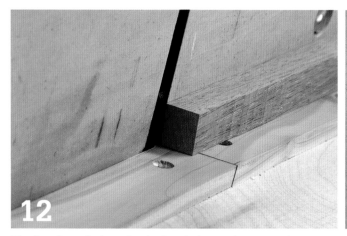

12

Here's a closer look at the slat in relation to the cutter. This is a safe and efficient operation.

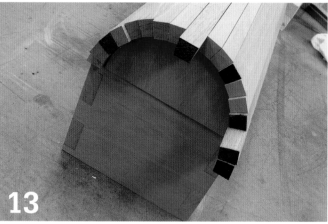

13

Cut 16 of the slats with bevels and put them temporarily on the end pieces. Then fit the last (top-center) slat.

14

Lay out all the top slats and tape them together.

15

Flip over the taped slats and apply glue to the bevel joints. Wrap this assembly around the top pieces and clamp it as shown, using the top end pieces as forms. Tape the edges of the top pieces to keep the glue from sticking to them.

16

When the slat assembly glue is dry, remove the clamps and scrape the inside of it to blend the slats into a smooth curve.

17

Cut the slat assembly to length. Then remove the tape from the ends and glue them to the slat assembly.

18

When the glue is dry, plane the slats into a smooth and continuous curve.

19

I made a jig to hold the lid while I sanded it. This gives you free access to the whole top.

20

Cut the top of the back of the box to accept the continuous hinge. This notch depth is the thickness of the hinge's barrel.

21

Install the hinge. Start by attaching the hinge to the box using one screw at each end of the hinge. Then attach the lid using one screw at each end of the hinge. Check the alignment of the lid with the box. If you need to make some adjustments, you can use the next screw hole on the hinge. Then, when the lid and box are properly aligned, you can install all of the screws in the hinge holes.

Cutting dovetails using the table saw

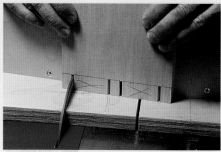

step one | Lay out the pins on the end and both faces of the piece. Draw a half pin on each side and add as many full pins as you like. Be sure to mark the waste material.

step two | Set the saw blade height to the thickness of the stock. Using the angled fence on the fixture, make your defining cuts for one side of the pins.

step three | Move the fixture to the other miter gauge slot, switch to the other angled fence and make the cuts on the other sides of the pins.

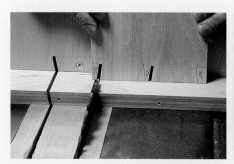

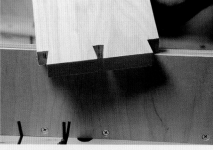

step four | Nibble away the waste between the pins with repeated passes over the blade. This is how the completed pins look.

step five | Use the pins as a template to lay out the tails. (Note pencil inside pin cavity.)

step six | Mark the waste material.

step seven | Tilt the blade to 10° and turn the fixture around so the straight fence faces the blade. Raise the blade to the material's thickness. Make the defining cuts on one side of each tail.

step eight | Flip the part face for face and make the defining cuts on the other side of the tails. Then clean out the waste.

step nine | Clean out the corners of the tails with a chisel.

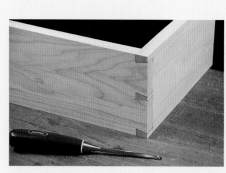

step ten | This joint fit together perfectly the first time it was cut. Practice will yield quick and accurate joinery every time.

inches (millimeters)

REFERENCE	QUANTITY	PART	STOCK	THICKNESS	(mm)	WIDTH	(mm)	LENGTH	(mm)
A	1	base	plywood	3/4	(19)	11 1/2	(292)	28	(711)
B	1	straight fence	plywood	3/4	(19)	4 1/2	(114)	28	(711)
C	1	straight mounting cleat	plywood	3/4	(19)	2	(51)	28	(711)
D	2	angled fences	plywood	3/4	(19)	4 1/2	(114)	14	(356)
E	2	angled mounting cleats	plywood	3/4	(19)	2	(51)	14	(356)
F	1	miter guide	plywood	3/8	(10)	3/4	(19)	13 1/2	(343)
G	4	blade guard blocks	plywood	1 1/2	(38)	2	(51)	3	(76)

Hardware & Supplies

29 #8 x 1 1/2" (38mm) flat-head wood screws

3 #6 x 3/4" (19mm) flat-head wood screws

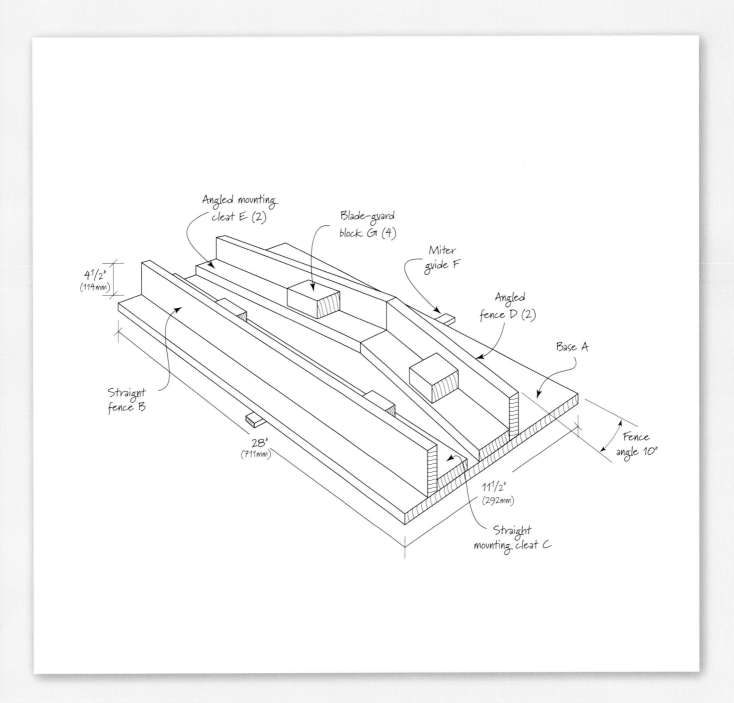

Angled mounting cleat E (2)

Blade-guard block G (4)

Miter guide F

Angled fence D (2)

Base A

4 1/2" (114mm)

Straight fence B

28" (711mm)

Fence angle 10°

11 1/2" (292mm)

Straight mounting cleat C

big top

HERE'S A PROJECT that will give you practice in laying out and cutting compound miters (gasp!). Before you panic and turn pages to the next project, give this one a chance. Yes, it looks like a circus tent, but that's because it's supposed to be a fun box.

You can use compound miters when installing mouldings or to impress people with your ability to think of two things (angles) at once. Just so you know, this project may not go together perfectly the first time

you cut the parts. Depending on your saw's gauges, your settings might not match mine exactly, and also, don't forget to account for wind velocity and relative humidity (just kidding).

When you make adjustments to make things fit better, make small changes because each change doubles when you cut a miter-to-miter joint.

You could keep your pet circus animals or pictures of clowns in this box. Or, fill it with peanuts.

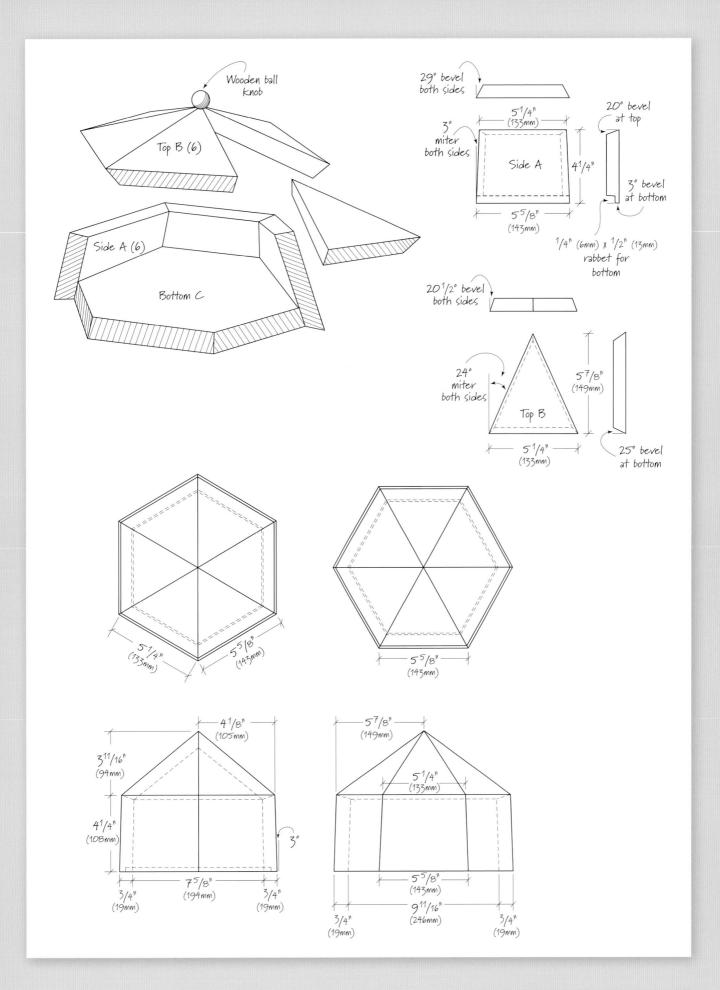

Wooden ball knob

Top B (6)

Side A (6)

Bottom C

29° bevel both sides

5¹/₄" (133mm)

3° miter both sides

Side A

4¹/₄"

5⁵/₈" (143mm)

20° bevel at top

3° bevel at bottom

1/4" (6mm) x 1/2" (13mm) rabbet for bottom

20¹/₂° bevel both sides

24° miter both sides

Top B

5⁷/₈" (149mm)

5¹/₄" (133mm)

25° bevel at bottom

5¹/₄" (133mm)

5⁵/₈" (143mm)

5⁵/₈" (143mm)

4¹/₈" (105mm)

3¹¹/₁₆" (94mm)

4¹/₄" (108mm)

3°

7⁵/₈" (194mm)

3/4" (19mm)

3/4" (19mm)

5⁷/₈" (149mm)

5¹/₄" (133mm)

5⁵/₈" (143mm)

9¹¹/₁₆" (246mm)

3/4" (19mm)

3/4" (19mm)

inches (millimeters)

REFERENCE	QUANTITY	PART	STOCK	THICKNESS	(mm)	WIDTH	(mm)	LENGTH	(mm)
A	6	sides	red oak	3/4	(19)	4 1/4	(108)	5 5/8	(143)
B	1	bottom	plywood	1/4	(6)	8 5/16	(211)	9 13/16	(249)
C	6	lid sides	red oak	3/4	(19)	5 1/4	(133)	5 7/8	(149)

Hardware & Supplies

1   1" diameter (25mm) wooden ball knob

1   pint oil base paint (your choice of color)

sanding sealer

finishing lacquer

Tools needed

table saw

power miter saw

jointer

2"-wide (51mm) masking tape

drill or screw gun

sliding T-bevel

combination square

tape ruler

120-, 150-, and 220-grit sandpapers or sanding discs

random-orbit sander

sanding block

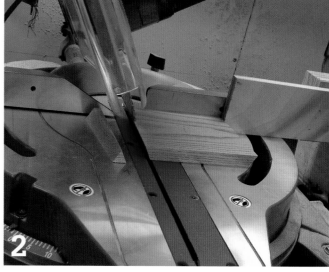

Rip a strip of oak long enough to yield six sides. Set your miter saw to a 3° miter and a 29° bevel. OK, here we go: Lay the oak strip on the saw bed, outside face down. Cut six pieces about ½" (13mm) longer than the finished dimensions. Put an X on each piece's top and inside edges as you cut them. I usually cut a couple of extra pieces just in case I mess up.

Don't change the saw's settings. Flip one of the side pieces and rotate it 180°. You don't want to see either of the X's you made. If you do see an X, orient the piece until you don't. Cut the piece to the final length. Don't move the part yet. Mark the location of its outer end and clamp a stop block at the mark. Now you can cut the rest of the parts accurately.

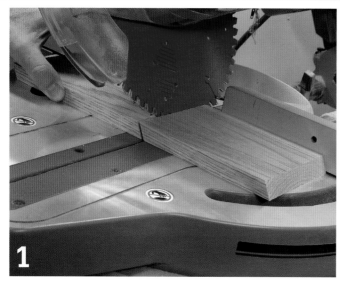

Set the fence on your jointer to 3° and cut a bevel on the bottoms of all sides. You should see the X on the top edge of the side; the other X should be against the fence.

Slide the fence toward the outside end of the cutter. Leave ⅜" (10mm) of cutter exposed. Lower the infeed table so you can make a ¼"-deep (6mm) cut. Now cut rabbets in all the bottom edges of the sides.

Cut a 20° bevel on the top edge of the sides. You'll cut off the X on the edge. The other X should be down on the saw's table. I used the table saw to cut this bevel but you could use the jointer. Also note that if you don't own or have access to a jointer, you can use the table saw to cut the bevels and rabbets on the bottoms of the sides.

Lay the sides, outside up, with the sharp edges of the miters touching each other. Apply tape at each of these joints. Fold the assembly together and see how well it all fits together — or not. You may need to fine-tune your miter cuts a bit to get things to come together correctly, but my directions and dimensions should bring you very close to acceptable.

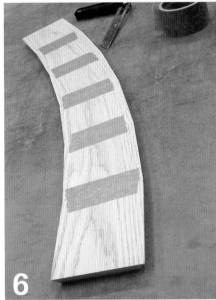

If everything is good to go, flip over the taped assembly and add glue to the miter joints. Fold it together and tape the last joint. Measure the distance to opposing joints: they should be equal. If not, tweak the assembly so they are. Then let the glue dry.

I've given the dimensions for the box bottom, but check the measurements of your box, which may not be exactly the same size as mine. Err on the side of slightly generous when you cut the bottom, then final fit it using a block plane.

Make this a nice fit and your family will marvel at your joint-making skills. If not, at least you know you've done your best. Don't glue the bottom into place just yet. First you'll add keys to strengthen the end-grain miter joints.

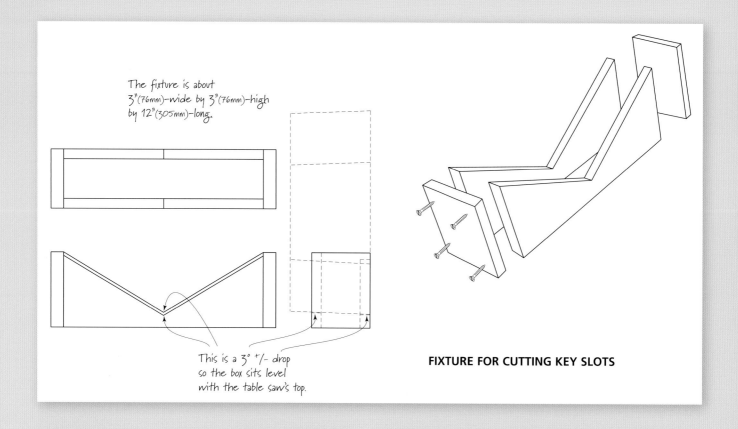

The fixture is about 3"(76mm)-wide by 3"(76mm)-high by 12"(305mm)-long.

This is a 3° +/- drop so the box sits level with the table saw's top.

FIXTURE FOR CUTTING KEY SLOTS

10

Make yourself a fixture like the one in the illustration above and use it to guide your box on the table saw. I know what you're thinking — Jim, don't you take chances using the table saw? No, I don't. This setup is stable, accurate and safe because the box covers the saw blade and the fence guides the fixture. If you don't feel comfortable using this method, make a similar setup using a router table. Do what feels and works best for you.

11

This is what you should have when the slots are cut. Notice that the top and bottom slots are equal distance from the top and bottom edges. The middle slot is located slightly above center. I thought it enhanced the look of the flared bottom of the box.

Cut some keys and glue them into the slots. Let the glue dry and trim the keys flush to the box. Get messy with the glue. It'll help fill in small gaps.

12

13

Make the lid parts a little larger than indicated in the cutting list. After the lid is assembled, it will need to be fitted to the box.

There's a couple of ways to cut compound miters. One is to make both the bevel and miter cuts at the same time. The other is to make the miter cut first, then cut the bevel. This is what I did for the lid parts because the miters come to a point at the top. This creates a problem if you try to make both cuts (the miter and bevel) at the same time on the miter saw. The first cut is OK but the second cut requires you to rotate and flip the piece (as you did with the box parts). Making this cut on the lid part will leave nothing on the part but a point at the fence. This leaves nothing to prevent the part from being jammed into the fence by the force of the rotating blade. I didn't like that scenario, so I cut the miters (no bevel) on each lid part using the two opposite miter settings on my miter saw. I kept the base of the lid part against the saw's fence and all was safe and sound. Then I used the band saw to cut the bevel on the lid parts. Tilt the saw's table to 20½°. Make a small sled and attach an angled stop block to it. Use this to guide the lid's parts past the band saw blade for one cut. Add another angled block to make the other bevel cut. If you make the sled wide enough, you can make one bevel cut on one side of the blade and the other bevel cut on the other side of the blade. It's up to you.

14

If necessary, smooth the band saw blade marks with a block plane. I found this made the joints fit almost watertight.

15

Lay out the parts, add tape and check the fit. Glue it up when you like what you see.

16

Cut the bevels on the bottom edges of the lid to fit into the bevel on the box. This may require a trial fit or two. After you finish the box, drill a hole in the center of the lid and use a 1¼" flat-head sheet metal screw to attach the wooden ball knob.

crazy 20

WHEN PEOPLE SEE THIS BOX they say, are you crazy? Well, I don't think I'm crazy — I may have a couple of screws loose but that's about it.

Once you get the parts cut out for this project, it's all about taping, gluing and folding it together. Then you apply the finish and you're done.

Having said that, it should be noted that the parts must be accurately cut. Only then will

it go together like it should. What will you learn from this project? More about cutting compound angles. I cut them using the same methods used for the lid of the Big Top project. The miter gets cut first, then the bevel. This saves you worrying about holding the parts safely in a table saw fixture or the miter saw. You can use the band saw to make the compound cut safely. However,

I found that cutting the miters on the table or miter saw made the cut much cleaner. Cutting the bevels on the band saw isn't as critical, so go for it. And let 'em call you crazy. We know something they don't. I just don't remember what it is. Is that crazy?

Oh, and just for the record, a 20-sided, three-dimensional spherical box like this is called an icosahedron.

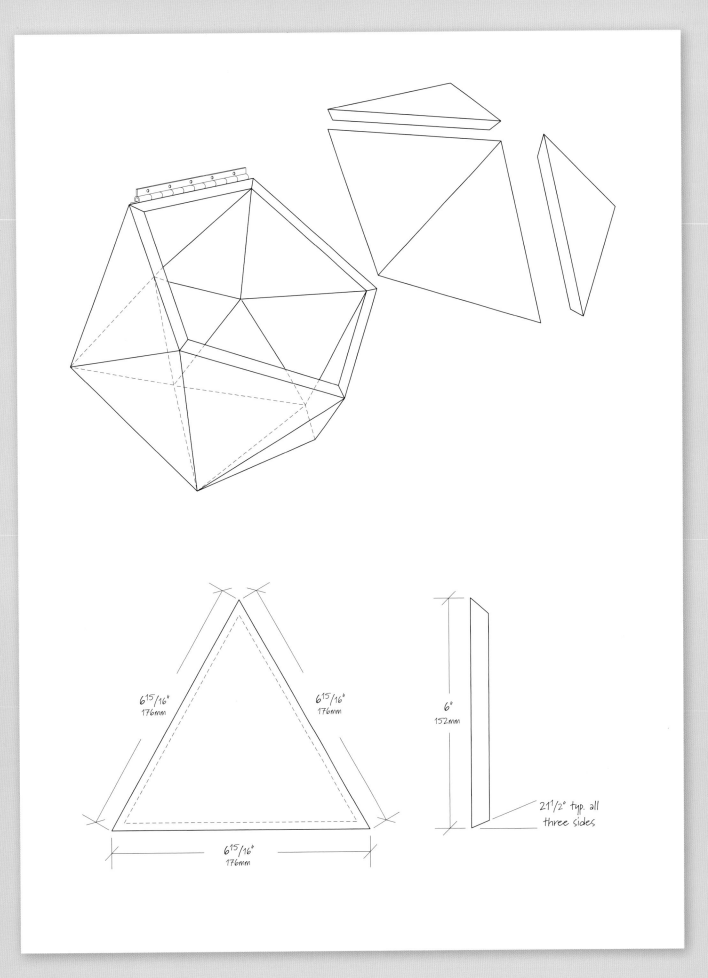

6^{15}/$_{16}$"
176mm

6^{15}/$_{16}$"
176mm

6^{15}/$_{16}$"
176mm

6"
152mm

21^{1}/$_{2}$° typ. all
three sides

inches (millimeters)

REFERENCE	QUANTITY	PART	STOCK	THICKNESS	(mm)	WIDTH	(mm)	LENGTH	(mm)
A	20	sides. tops, bottoms, etc.	birch plywood	1/2	(13)	7	(178)	11	(279)

Hardware & Supplies

10 No. 8-1 1/2" x 14 3/4" (38mm x 375mm) wood screws

8 No. 6 - 3/4" (19mm) wood screws

12 6d finish nails

drywall spackling

paint color of your choice

Tools needed

table saw or power miter saw

band saw

drill ("egg beater" style or handheld electric)

3/32" (2mm) twist drill

Phillips screwdriver

60-, 100-, 120-, 150- and 220-grit sandpapers

No. 0000 steel wool

sanding block (see sanding block sidebar page 11)

random-orbit electric sander (optional)

Start by ripping several lengths of plywood to the width of the height of the parts. Then set the table saw's miter gauge to 60°. Cut the angle on the end of the ripped blank.

Set up a stop on the miter gauge's fence. This will require some trial and error. Each side of the triangles must be exactly the same length. When you've got this fine-tuned, you're ready to start cutting sides. After you've cut the angle on the end of the blank, turn it face down and push the corner against the stop. Keep doing this until you run out of material. Go to the next blank and cut more sides. You'll need 20 sides in all. I usually cut five extra in case I mess up. It happens to the best of us.

Here's one method of cutting the bevels on the sides. Set your band saw fence to the correct bevel angle (see the illustration), make a sled that fits on the table and attach a fence at 30° to the fence of the sled. When you hold one side against the fence, it should line up the adjacent side as shown. You can then push the sled and the part past the saw blade. As an option, you can also use a power miter saw or table saw, but those large turning blades have a tendency to grab material when cutting bevels. You're cutting a compound angle one angle at time. In my experience, it's safer to make the cuts one at at time when working with small parts. If one of these little parts gets away from you, it opens up the possibility of injury to your fingers or hands. It's not worth taking a chance.

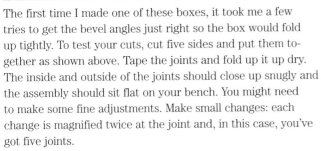

The first time I made one of these boxes, it took me a few tries to get the bevel angles just right so the box would fold up tightly. To test your cuts, cut five sides and put them together as shown above. Tape the joints and fold up it up dry. The inside and outside of the joints should close up snugly and the assembly should sit flat on your bench. You might need to make some fine adjustments. Make small changes: each change is magnified twice at the joint and, in this case, you've got five joints.

When you've got it all working, tape the box in the configuration shown in step 4. Turn the whole thing over and apply glue to all of the joints. Fold it together and add tape to the open joints. Obviously, you'll be gluing up the lid separately. It's a cool thing to see this whole thing fold up and come together. One second it's flat and the next it's a 15-sided box with a 5-sided lid!

The hinge is surface-mounted on the outside of the box and is painted to match the box. Finish-sand to 220-grit sandpaper. Apply primer that is compatible with the paint you'll be using. If you don't apply primer, there is a good chance the paint won't cure properly. Years ago, I was finishing a tabletop that I had made of MDF. After I shaped and sanded the top, I applied the colored finishing lacquer. The lacquer wouldn't cure and remained soft, even after I waited several days. I had to remove the finish and use the recommended primer first. When the finish lacquer was applied over the primer, it cured to a nice hard finish. Lesson learned the hard way. One other great thing about primer is that it has a lot of solids in it. After you apply a couple of coats, you can sand it using 320-grit sandpaper and achieve an amazingly smooth surface. If there are any dings still left, you can fill them with spackling, sand and apply more primer. Keep doing this until you like the way the surface looks. Then apply the paint. It will flow so smoothly, you'll be amazed. Top coat with a clear lacquer. Be sure the clear top coat won't wrinkle or react with the paint. Make a test piece to be sure.

13

BAND-SAWN BOXES are made from a chunk of wood. The idea is that the box already exists in the block and you just remove material to reveal it. So find a block of wood you like or glue a few pieces of wood together to make a block.

I thought it would be interesting to make a box that is similar in shape to a bentwood Shaker box but made primarily using the band saw. The techniques used to make this box can be used to make any shape or size box. You could make this box without the drawer, an easier project. Then, with the block you have left, you could make another smaller box.

When making a band-sawn box, you need to think inside the box and plan your cuts carefully. This project teaches you to visualize how the parts (lid, bottom, outside, drawer) relate to each other. Before you cut any wood, study the drawing and see where each part is located. Then you'll start to see it's not as complicated as it might seem at first glance.

You can fill this box with scented potpourri or jewelry.

almost in
the round

76

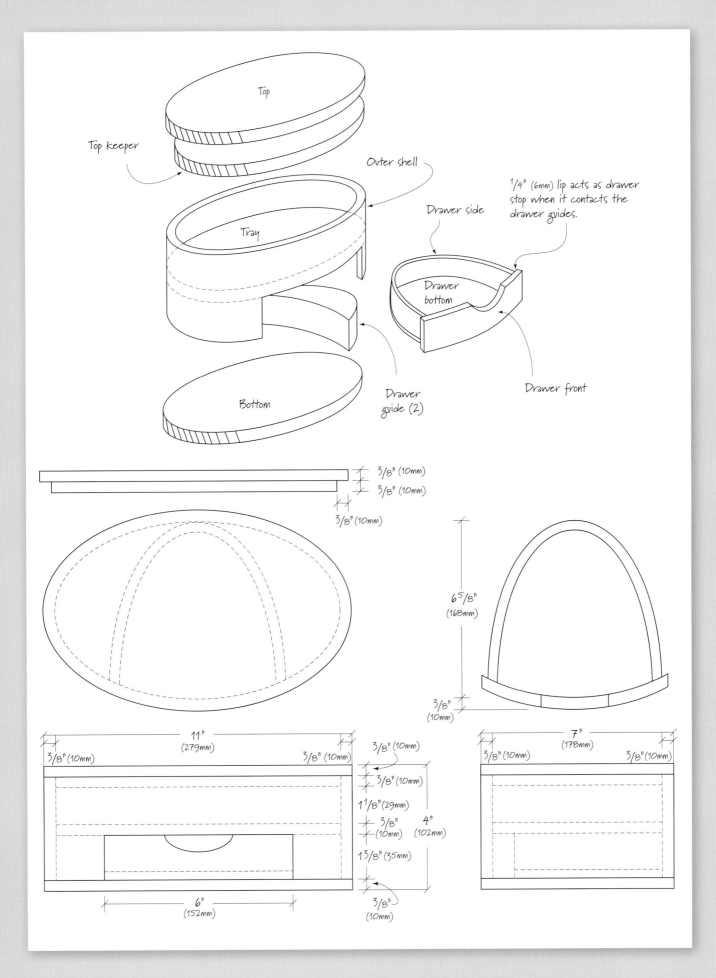

Top

Top keeper

Outer shell

Tray

1/4" (6mm) lip acts as drawer stop when it contacts the drawer guides.

Drawer side

Drawer bottom

Drawer guide (2)

Drawer front

Bottom

3/8" (10mm)
3/8" (10mm)
3/8" (10mm)

6⁵/₈"
(168mm)

3/8"
(10mm)

11"
(279mm)

3/8" (10mm)

3/8" (10mm)

3/8" (10mm)

3/8" (10mm)

1¹/₈" (29mm)

3/8" (10mm)

4"
(102mm)

1³/₈" (35mm)

6"
(152mm)

3/8"
(10mm)

7"
(178mm)

3/8"(10mm)

3/8"(10mm)

inches (millimeters)

REFERENCE	QUANTITY	PART	STOCK	THICKNESS	(mm)	WIDTH	(mm)	LENGTH	(mm)
A	1	block of wood	cherry	4	(102)	7½	(191)	11	(279)

Hardware & Supplies

spray or wipe on lacquer

Tools needed

band saw

sanding block

random-orbit electric sander

stationary sander (optional)

60-, 100-, 120-, 150- and 220-grit sandpapers

No. 0000 steel wool

Make a template of the box shape. Plywood or MDF is the best material for making templates because it won't change shape with the seasons.

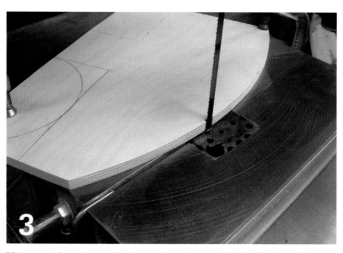

Take your time and make the pattern the exact shape you'd like your finished box to be. You can use a stationary sander or hold the template in a vise and shape it with a sanding block.

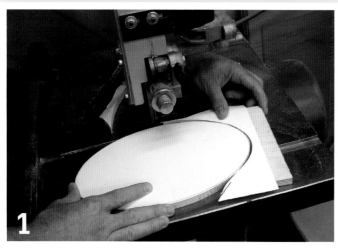

Using another piece of plywood, make a guide for the template. Cut a curve on one edge and cut a notch to fit around the band saw blade. Clamp the guide to the band saw table so the curved edge of the guide is flush to the outside of the band saw blade.

CUTTING ORDER FOR BANDSAWN BOX

1. Cut ellipse from box block.

2. Cut bottom from ellipse block.

3. Cut top from ellipse block.

4. Cut inner block from ellipse, leaving outer shell.

5. Cut lid keeper from top of inner block.

6. Cut tray from inner block.

7. Cut drawer block from remaining inner block.

8. Cut drawer bottom from drawer block.

9. Cut drawer side from drawer block, leaving inner drawer block.

10. Cut drawer front from outer box shell.

This photo shows how the guide should be set in relation to the band saw blade. The box template will ride against the edge of the guide as the saw blade cuts the box block to shape.

I use a small wax candle to reduce the friction on the band saw table. Products that come in a spray can are also excellent for keeping your saw's table slick. Check your local hardware store.

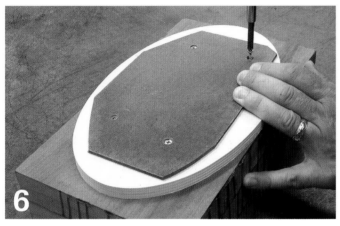

Attach the box template to the bottom of your box blank. Add a 1/8"-thick (3mm) spacer to the bottom of the template. This spacer makes sure the box blank clears the guide on the saw table.

Before making any cuts, write down each cutting step in the order they're to be done. (See sidebar, "Cutting Order for Band-sawn Box".) If you don't do this, you could easily get the order mixed up and that's frustrating, because it means you've ruined your box blank and you'll need to start over!

Hold the box template against the guide. Then cut the box blank to shape. I recommend you practice with scrap material until you're comfortable. Then go for it.

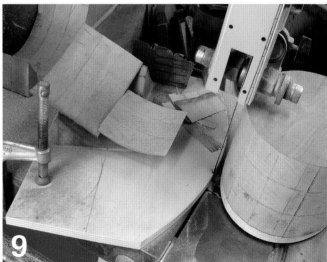

This is another view of the setup. You can copy any shape you like using this setup on your band saw. The key is a sharp blade and a slow, steady feed of the material past the saw blade.

Sand the box blank smooth before making more saw cuts.

Set the saw's fence and cut the lid and bottom from the box blank.

PUT PENCIL MARK HERE ON THE FENCE BEHIND THE BLADE

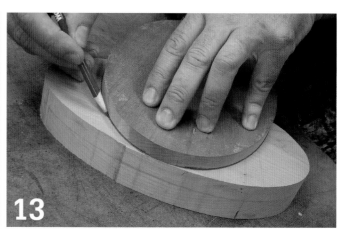

Cut the outside of the box from the blank. Make the entrance cut parallel to the wood's grain direction, then make the cut using the saw's fence as your guide. I find it helpful to make a pencil mark that lines up with the saw blade on the saw's fence. Keep pressure at this point on the fence with the box blank. Again, practice this technique using scrap material until you're comfortable with the process.

Slice the remaining box blank material to the thickness of the drawer. Trace the shape of the drawer on this blank. The drawer may be square or oval, as I've chosen. I used one end of the box lid as a template. Cut the drawer from this blank.

Reset the band saw fence and, using the same technique you used in step 12, cut the drawer bottom from the blank . Then cut the drawer side from the drawer blank. Glue the drawer side to the drawer bottom, and glue the entrance cut on the box together.

Use the two blocks leftover from the drawer blank as drawer guides. Place them inside the box side and mark the location of the drawer.

Transfer the marks to the front of the drawer side. Make sure the drawer front is ¼" longer than between the marks. Cut the drawer front from the box's side. I found it helpful to clamp a straightedge to guide the saw. Start this cut on the outside of the box side and cut through the side. After you've cut through the side, plunge the saw through the cut and cut cleanly to each edge of the drawer front.

Here's a closer look at the start of the plunge cut. Note the triangle pencil mark showing which end is up on the side.

I used the box tray to hold the shape of the box side while I finished cutting the drawer front.

Glue the drawer guide blanks to the tray and box's side

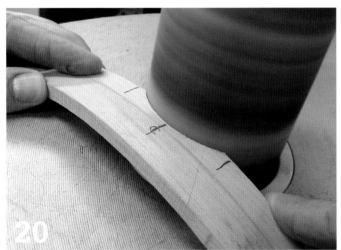

Cut or sand a finger pull into the drawer front. As an alternative, you could add a drawer pull to the drawer front.

Glue the drawer front to the drawer. Use spacers inside the box to take up the space between the tray and the lid keeper. Set the lid keeper in the box on top of the spacers, add glue to the top of the lid keeper and set the lid on top of it. Use clamps to hold the lid in place until the glue dries. Sand the box with the lid and drawer in place. Finish-sand using 220-grit sandpaper.

14

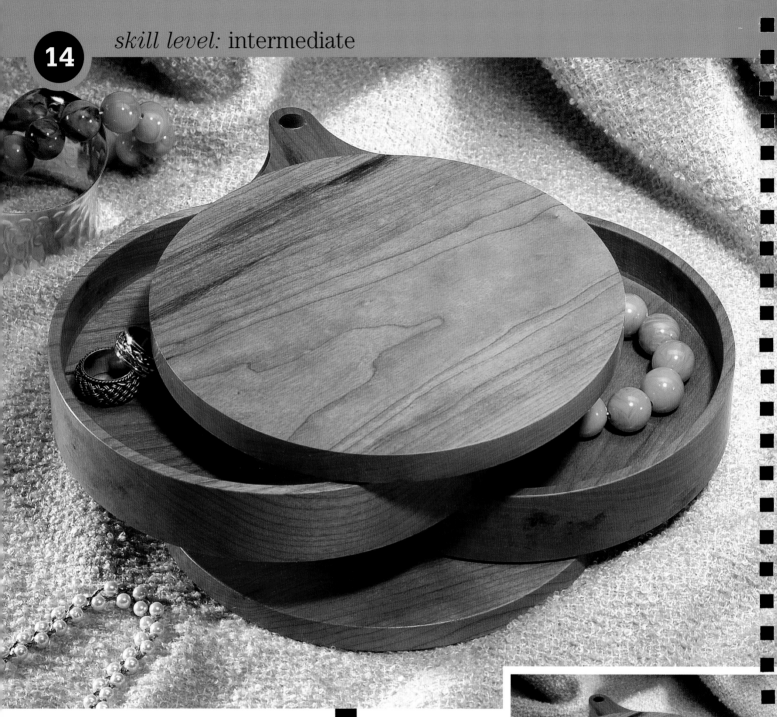

roundup

MMM, ROUND THINGS PILED ON TOP OF EACH OTHER — I think I'll call this one roundup. This project takes up where "almost in the round" left off. The same outer-ring cutting techniques apply to cutting these circle boxes.

I'm sure a lot of woodworkers have used this ring-cutting technique but I discovered it by accident. I was making a round tabletop and it was a little too big in diameter the first time I cut it out. So I made an entrance cut and removed a ¾"-thick (19mm) ring from the top. I saved the ring because it looked cool; and later made a round mirror frame out of it.

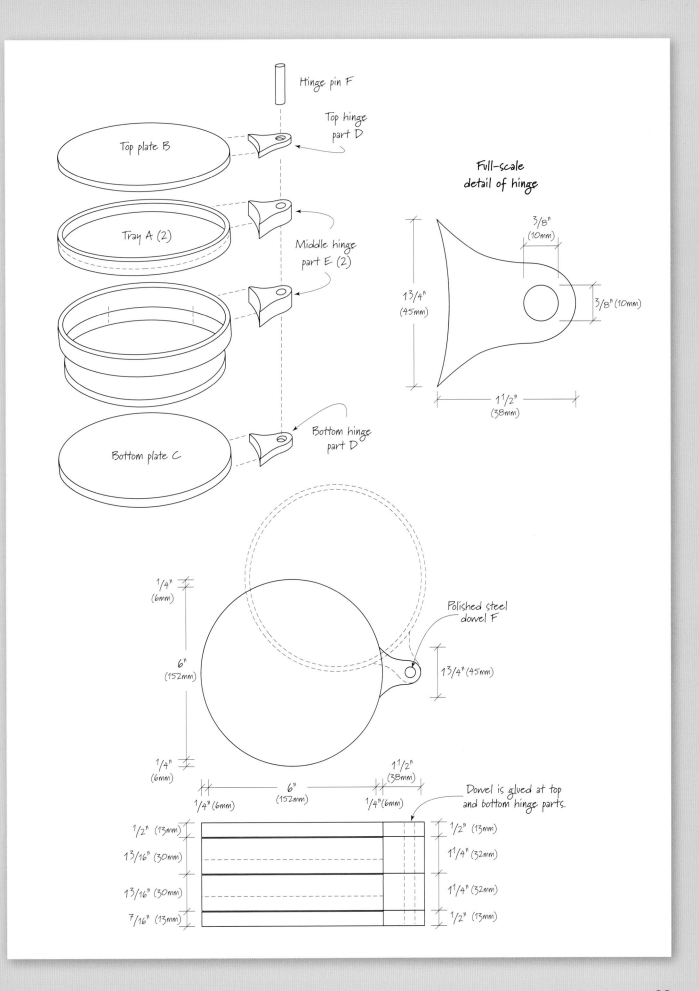

Hinge pin F

Top hinge part D

Top plate B

Full-scale detail of hinge

Tray A (2)

Middle hinge part E (2)

3/8" (10mm)

1 3/4" (45mm)

3/8" (10mm)

1 1/2" (38mm)

Bottom plate C

Bottom hinge part D

Polished steel dowel F

1/4" (6mm)

6" (152mm)

13/4" (45mm)

1/4" (6mm)

1 1/2" (38mm)

6" (152mm)

1/4"(6mm)

1/4"(6mm)

Dowel is glued at top and bottom hinge parts.

1/2" (13mm)

13/16" (30mm)

13/16" (30mm)

7/16" (13mm)

1/2" (13mm)

1 1/4" (32mm)

1 1/4" (32mm)

1/2" (13mm)

inches (millimeters)

REFERENCE	QUANTITY	PART	STOCK	THICKNESS	(mm)	WIDTH	(mm)	LENGTH	(mm)
A	2	trays	cherry	$1\frac{3}{16}$	(30)	$6\frac{1}{2}$ dia.(165)			
B	1	top plate	cherry	$\frac{1}{2}$	(13)	$6\frac{1}{2}$ dia.(165)			
C	1	bottom plate	cherry	$\frac{7}{16}$	(11)	$6\frac{1}{2}$ dia.(165)			
D	2	top/bottom hinge parts	cherry	$\frac{1}{2}$	(13)	$1\frac{1}{2}$	(38)	$1\frac{3}{4}$	(45)
E	2	middle hinge parts	cherry	$1\frac{1}{4}$	(32)	$1\frac{1}{2}$	(38)	$1\frac{3}{4}$	(45)
F	1	hinge pin	steel	$\frac{3}{8}$ dia. (10)				$3\frac{1}{2}$	(89)

Tools needed

band saw

stationary disc sander

oscillating-spindle sander

sanding block

random-orbit electric sander

60-, 100-, 120-, 150-, 220-, 400-, 600- and 1200-grit sandpapers

No. 0000 steel wool

Hardware & Supplies

spray or wipe-on lacquer

inches (millimeters)

REFERENCE	QUANTITY	PART	THICKNESS	(mm)	WIDTH	(mm)	LENGTH	(mm)
A	1	base	$\frac{3}{4}$	(19)	12	(305)	18	(457)
B	2	top plates	$\frac{1}{2}$	(13)	$5\frac{3}{4}$	(146)	3	(76)
C	1	sliding arm	$\frac{1}{2}$	(13)	$1\frac{3}{8}$	(35)	18	(457)
D	1	cleat	$\frac{3}{4}$	(19)	2	(51)	12	(305)
E	1	runner	$\frac{3}{8}$	(10)	$\frac{3}{4}$	(19)	15	(381)

Hardware & Supplies

1 $1\frac{1}{2}$" x $\frac{1}{4}$" -20 (38mm x 6mm-20) finger bolt

1 $\frac{1}{4}$" -20 (6mm x 25mm) T-nut

1 $\frac{1}{4}$" x 1" (6mm x 25mm) dowel

1 penny (any minting date will work!)

1

Use a circle-cutting fixture attached to your band saw to cut the top, bottom and trays. After drilling the pivot hole, lay the blank on the jig and insert the pivot pin into the pivot hole.

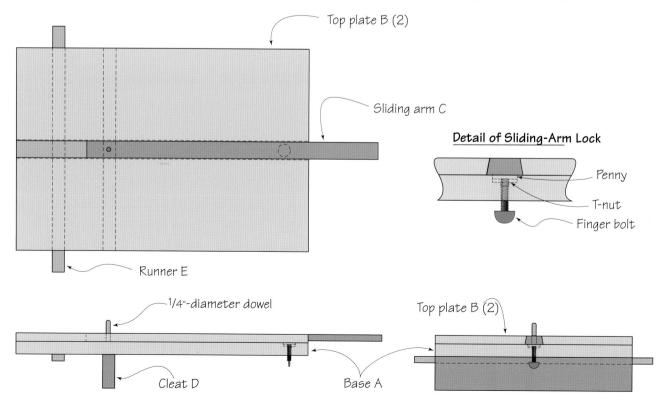

Top plate B (2)

Sliding arm C

Runner E

Detail of Sliding-Arm Lock

Penny

T-nut

Finger bolt

1/4"-diameter dowel

Cleat D

Base A

Top plate B (2)

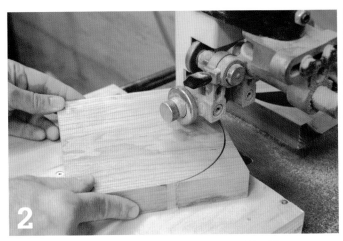

With the saw blade snug against one of the blank's sides, cut the circle. Don't rush the cutting — let the blade do the work.

Find a dark streak in the wood grain where you can make the entrance cuts to start the ring-cutting process. Also, mark the bottom of the blank so you'll know where to locate the ring at glueup time.

Reset the circle-cutting fixture's pivot pin and cut the rings. When the entrance cut is glued together, it will almost disappear because it will blend with the wood grain.

This is a slick technique! When the entrance cut is glued together, it will close the ring just enough to compensate for the thickness of the saw-blade kerf and the ring will fit snugly around the tray. I love it when a plan comes together.

Set the saw's fence and cut the trays to thickness. Sand the inside of the tray before glue up. You'll be glad you did.

7

You can use your oscillating-spindle sander to lightly sand the inside of the rings to remove the saw blade marks. Then glue the rings to the trays. When the ring is pulled together and the clamp is applied at the entrance cut, you won't need any clamps to tighten the ring to the tray. It's magic!

8

I glued the hinge-part blanks temporarily together by inserting paper in the glue joints. This will ensure they are cut to the same size and shape. When you're done shaping the hinge pieces, they can easily be pried apart.

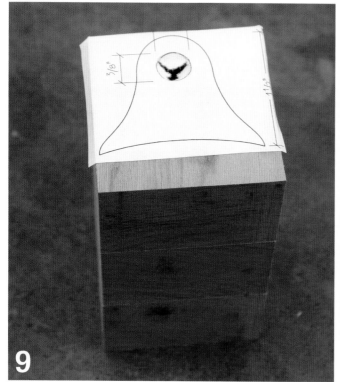

9

Drill the hole for the hinge pin. Make a copy of the full-size pivot-hinge pattern and attach it to the hinge-part blank assembly.

10

Cut the hinge parts to shape. Feed the work slowly and you'll easily make the curved cuts.

11

Use your spindle sander to fine-tune the fit of the hinge parts to the tray's bottom and top. Then finish smoothing and shaping the hinge parts.

12

Separate the hinge parts and glue them to their respective top, bottom and trays. The hinge parts for the trays and bottom are slightly thicker than the parts to which they're attached. This ensures the parts won't scrape each other when you open and close the trays.

13

I used the unthreaded part of a machine bolt shaft for the hinge pin. I polished the top of the pin using progressively finer grits of sandpaper, finishing up with 1200-grit sandpaper. Finish the parts before final assembly. Then use two-part epoxy to fasten the bottom and top plates to the hinge pin. Use waxed paper to keep the epoxy off the other parts. Make sure the parts are lined up correctly and that everything is straight. You have about 5 minutes of working time with the epoxy.

14

The polished head of the steel looks nice against the cherry wood. A brass or bronze rod would look great as well.

A FRENCH-CURVE drawing template inspired this project. The French curve is a fixed shape that has been used for years as a basic starting point for designs using complex curves. The shape is smooth, pleasing to look at and has a natural flow. However, I don't have a clue as to why it's called a *French* curve, as opposed to, say, a Nebraska or Walla Walla curve. The techniques for making the box are borrowed from *Building Beautiful Boxes with Your Band Saw* by Lois Keener Ventura, published by F+W Publications.

As the name of this project suggests, it is advisable to slow down when making tight, curved cuts on the band saw. It's a nice way of using a power tool. Relax, let the tool do the work and you'll be amazed at the results.

You'll learn about the band saw and what it can do. Also, you'll learn how to finish-sand. Shaping and sanding this project is more complicated than sanding a flat panel. A medium-cut wood rasp and a smooth-cut file will help with the general shaping of edges and getting into tight spots. You'll also use a sharp chisel. The box requires that you finish-sand to a final grit of 220. This takes some patience on your part but the results are worth it. It's a treat to watch the grain of the wood appear before your eyes as you remove the sanding scratches from grit to finer grit. Remember, take it slow on the curves.

watch out for
the curves

inches (millimeters)

REFERENCE	QUANTITY	PART	STOCK	THICKNESS	(mm)	WIDTH	(mm)	LENGTH	(mm)
A	1	wooden blank	cherry	4 1/2	(114)	6	(152)	10	(254)

Hardware & Supplies

3   3/16" x 1/2" (5mm x 13mm) brass rods

spray or rub-on lacquer

Tools needed

drill ("egg beater" style or handheld electric)

3/16" (5mm) twist drill

60-, 100-, 120-, 150- and 220-grit sandpapers

No. 0000 steel wool

sanding block

random-orbit electric sander

band saw

spindle sander

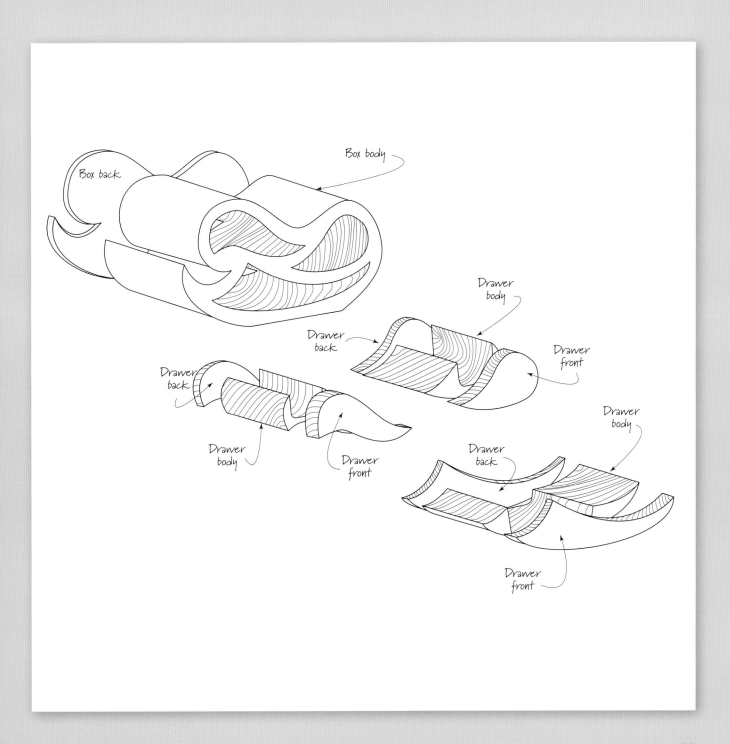

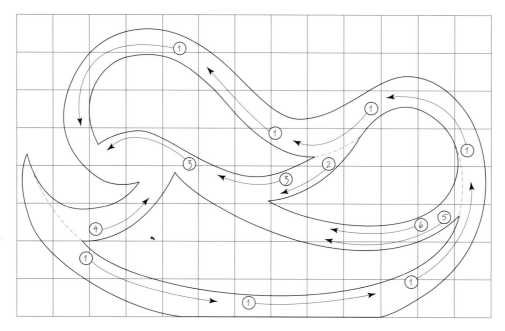

Each square represents 10mm   Enlarge 200% for full-scale template.

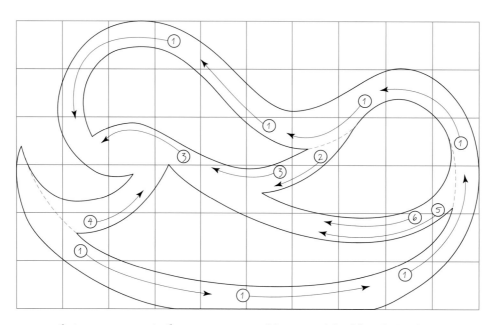

Each square represents 1"   Enlarge 200% for full-scale template.

1

After you clamp up your box blank, let the glue dry at least 24 hours. I used one board of 12-year-old cherry for this box. I had forgotten I even had the board — maybe I need to clean out my wood rack. Make a copy of the box pattern (or make up your own pattern) and, using spray adhesive, stick it to your glued up box blank.

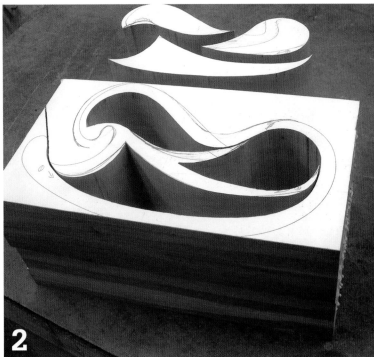

2

Note the order of making the cuts using numbers and arrows. If you used the supplied pattern, the arrows are already drawn and numbered for you. Make the first cut and take your time doing it. Then stop at the end of the cut and shut off the saw. Move the box into position for the next cut. You'll have to maneuver the box so the stopped saw blade can back up in the saw kerf. Start the saw, make the second cut, then stop, shut off the saw and remaneuver for the next cut, etc. This takes some time, so don't hurry. Enjoy the moment.

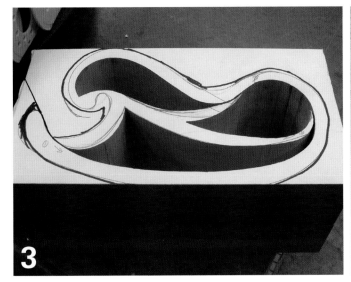

3

My band saw blade is ³⁄₈" (10mm) wide, so I couldn't make the cuts as tight as the pattern that I drew. I went with the flow and cut what the saw told me to cut. No worries. I simply drew a different outside cutting line to match the inside curves that I cut. I would recommend a ³⁄₁₆"- or ¼"-wide (5mm or 6mm) saw blade to make these boxes. Whatever size blade you use, be sure it's sharp!

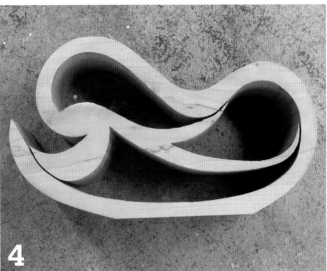

4

Here's the final rough shape of the box.

5

I'm not telling you to go out and buy a new sander but a stationary disc or belt sander comes in handy here. Smooth the outside curves.

6

You'll need an oscillating-spindle sander to smooth the inside curves. In this case, I recommend you buy one of these really cool sanders.

7

Cut the backs and fronts off the drawer blanks.

8

Insert the remaining drawer blanks inside the box. Use a square to help you make the vertical cutout marks for the drawers.

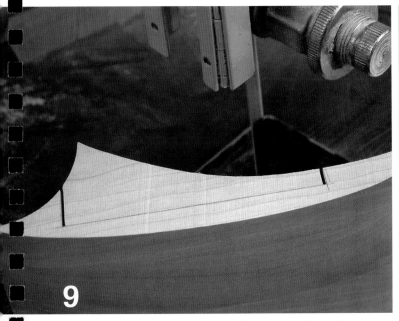

9

Connect the vertical cutout lines with horizontal lines. Make the vertical cuts first.

10

Make half of the horizontal cut, connecting it to one of the vertical cuts.

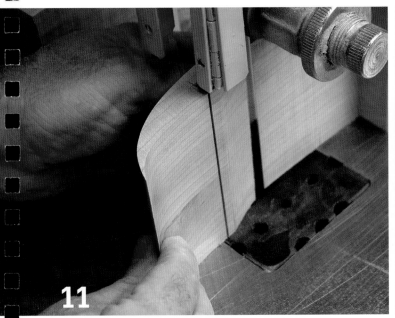

11

Make the second half of the horizontal cut to connect the vertical cuts.

12

Ta da! Now you have a drawer with a bottom and sides.

13

Sand the insides of the drawer backs and fronts to remove any marks the band saw made. Then reattach the drawer fronts and backs with glue.

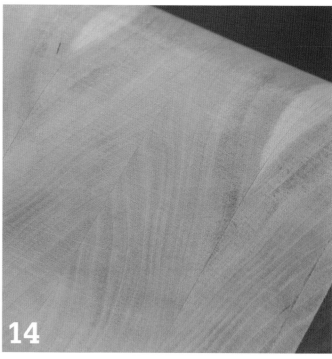

14

Now comes the part that determines whether this project will turn out just so-so or top of the line. Yes, I'm talking about sanding. Though the spindle and disc sanders sanded things pretty smoothly, if you look closely, you can see scratch marks. Time to break out the sandpaper and some sanding blocks.

15

I used 220-grit sandpaper and sanded across the grain to speed up the scratch removal process. If you're using a finer-grit sandpaper like this, you can get away with sanding across the grain to get things leveled out. But we're not done yet.

16

I cut off an 8" (203mm) section of a broom handle and wrapped it with part of an old cotton towel. Then I wrapped some fresh 220-grit sandpaper around it. The hardwood broom handle isn't perfectly flat and chances are the box isn't either. The towel backer lets the sandpaper conform to the imperfections. I'm not talking about large imperfections — I'm talking about a few thousands of an inch here and there.

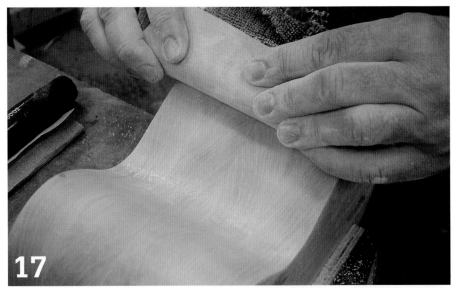

Sand with the grain of the wood. This can take some time but it will be worth it. As you sand, frequently brush the dust away and check your progress. You should begin to see the grain of the wood. You're polishing the surface of the wood and those coarse scratches are being replaced by finer ones.

17

18

Use a chisel or knife to smooth the sharp edges in tight spots. It goes without saying that these tools should be sharp.

19

Fit sandpaper between tight spaces and blend the roundover of the edges into the rest of the box.

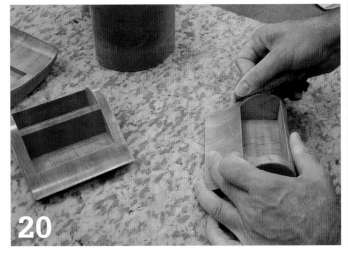

20

I finish-sanded using 220-grit sandpaper and applied a lacquer finish. After the lacquer cured, I rubbed the parts with #0000 steel wool. This smoothed things quite nicely. If you want, you can line the drawers with flocking. I chose to let the wood show.

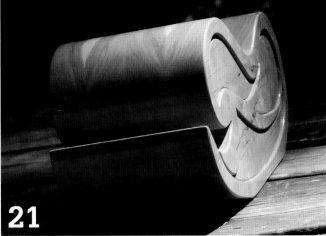

21

Some woods change color quickly as they are exposed to sunlight. I sat the box in the sun for an afternoon and it gave the wood a quick-aged patina — not a lot, but it was noticeably darker. It looked good for the photo shoot.

there's no point

THIS ONE IS CALLED "There's No Point" because the top doesn't come to a point. Maybe it should be called "Pyramid Power" or "Why Didn't You Just Make the Box Square So the Drawers Would Be Easier to Make?"

This drawer box has lots of room for jewelry, birthday cards or a prized set of socket drivers.

(It would make a conversation-starting toolbox!)

The body is veneered, and the veneer wraps itself around the box in one continuous grain pattern. You'll use your biscuit joiner to make this box. Also, you'll learn to make fitted drawers (drawers that are fitted to the opening of the cabinet — no hardware needed) that

use the drawer bottoms as runners. The drawer style isn't new, but it is easy to make (well, it's easy to make when the drawers are square). You can use the techniques to make a larger cabinet or toolbox with drawers — the cool part being you don't have to buy, or deal with, mechanical drawer glides.

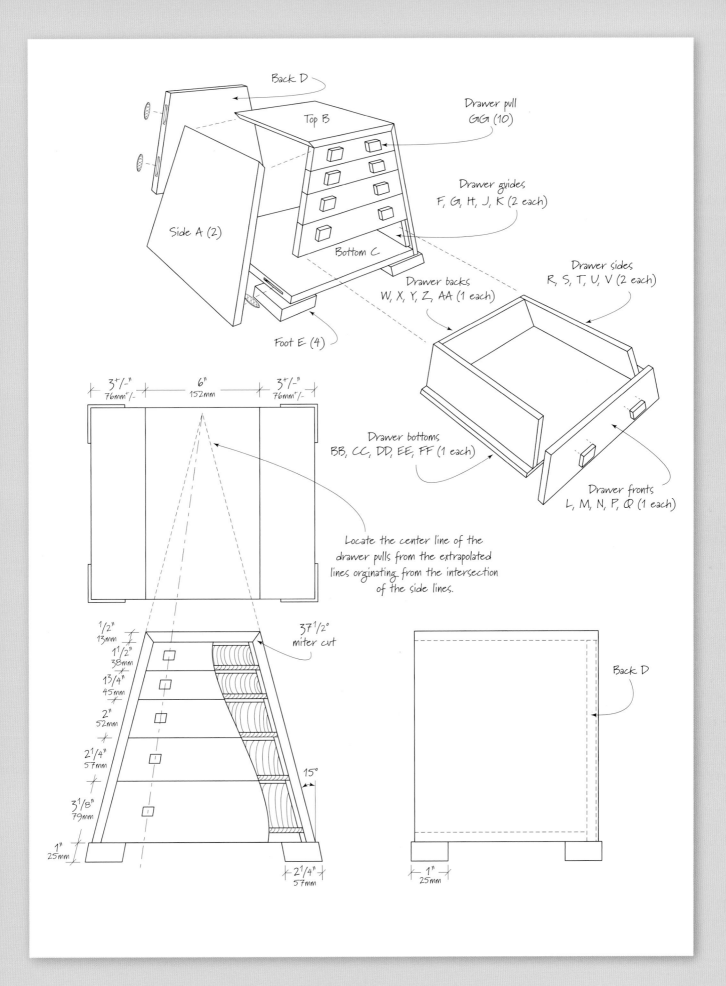

Back D

Drawer pull
GG (10)

Top B

Drawer guides
F, G, H, J, K (2 each)

Side A (2)

Bottom C

Drawer sides
R, S, T, U, V (2 each)

Drawer backs
W, X, Y, Z, AA (1 each)

Foot E (4)

Drawer bottoms
BB, CC, DD, EE, FF (1 each)

Drawer fronts
L, M, N, P, Q (1 each)

3⁺/-"
76mm⁺/-   6"
152mm   3⁺/-"
76mm⁺/-

Locate the center line of the
drawer pulls from the extrapolated
lines orginating from the intersection
of the side lines.

1/2"
13mm

1¹/2"
38mm

1³/4"
45mm

2"
52mm

2¹/4"
57mm

3¹/8"
79mm

1"
25mm

37¹/2°
miter cut

15°

2¹/4"
57mm

Back D

1"
25mm

97

inches (millimeters)

REFERENCE	QUANTITY	PART	STOCK	THICKNESS	(mm)	WIDTH	(mm)	LENGTH	(mm)	
A	2	sides	veneered ply	$\frac{1}{2}$	(13)	10	(254)	$11\frac{1}{2}$	(292)	length includes miters
B	1	top	veneered ply	$\frac{1}{2}$	(13)	10	(254)	6	(152)	length includes miters
C	1	bottom	plywood	$\frac{1}{2}$	(13)	$9\frac{1}{8}$	(232)	11 +/-	(279)	
D	1	back	veneered ply	$\frac{1}{2}$	(13)	$10\frac{5}{8}$ H	(270)	11 +/-	(279)	veneer grain runs horizontally
E	4	feet	maple	1	(25)	$2\frac{1}{4}$	(57)	$2\frac{1}{4}$	(57)	
F	2	drawer guides	plywood	$\frac{1}{4}$	(6)	$2\frac{1}{2}$	(64)	$9\frac{1}{8}$	(232)	15° bevel on two long edges
G	2	drawer guides	plywood	$\frac{1}{4}$	(6)	$2\frac{1}{8}$	(54)	$9\frac{1}{8}$	(232)	15° bevel on two long edges
H	2	drawer guides	plywood	$\frac{1}{4}$	(6)	$1\frac{7}{8}$	(48)	$9\frac{1}{8}$	(232)	15° bevel on two long edges
J	2	drawer guides	plywood	$\frac{1}{4}$	(6)	$1\frac{5}{8}$	(41)	$9\frac{1}{8}$	(232)	15° bevel on two long edges
K	2	drawer guides	plywood	$\frac{1}{4}$	(6)	$1\frac{3}{8}$	(35)	$9\frac{1}{8}$	(232)	15° bevel on two long edges
L	2	drawer fronts	veneered ply	$\frac{1}{2}$	(13)	3	(76)	9	(229)	15° miter on both ends
M	2	drawer fronts	veneered ply	$\frac{1}{2}$	(13)	$2\frac{1}{4}$	(57)	9	(229)	15° miter on both ends
N	2	drawer fronts	veneered ply	$\frac{1}{2}$	(13)	$1\frac{15}{16}$	(49)	9	(229)	15° miter on both ends
P	2	drawer fronts	veneered ply	$\frac{1}{2}$	(13)	$1\frac{11}{16}$	(43)	9	(229)	15° miter on both ends
Q	2	drawer fronts	veneered ply	$\frac{1}{2}$	(13)	$1\frac{7}{16}$	(37)	9	(229)	15° miter on both ends
R	2	drawer sides	poplar	$\frac{1}{2}$	(13)	$2\frac{3}{8}$	(60)	9	(229)	15° bevel on two long edges
S	2	drawer sides	poplar	$\frac{1}{2}$	(13)	2	(51)	9	(229)	15° bevel on two long edges
T	2	drawer sides	poplar	$\frac{1}{2}$	(13)	$1\frac{3}{4}$	(45)	9	(229)	15° bevel on two long edges
U	2	drawer sides	poplar	$\frac{1}{2}$	(13)	$1\frac{3}{8}$	(35)	9	(229)	15° bevel on two long edges
V	2	drawer sides	poplar	$\frac{1}{2}$	(13)	$1\frac{1}{4}$	(32)	9	(229)	15° bevel on two long edges
W	1	drawer back	poplar	$\frac{1}{2}$	(13)	$2\frac{3}{8}$	(60)	9	(229)	15° bevel on both ends
X	1	drawer back	poplar	$\frac{1}{2}$	(13)	$1\frac{15}{16}$	(49)	9	(229)	15° bevel on both ends
Y	1	drawer back	poplar	$\frac{1}{2}$	(13)	$1\frac{11}{16}$	(43)	9	(229)	15° bevel on both ends
Z	1	drawer back	poplar	$\frac{1}{2}$	(13)	$1\frac{1}{2}$	(38)	9	(229)	15° bevel on both ends
AA	1	drawer back	poplar	$\frac{1}{2}$	(13)	$1\frac{1}{4}$	(32)	9	(229)	15° bevel on both ends
BB	1	drawer bottom	plywood	$\frac{1}{4}$	(6)	$10\frac{11}{16}$	(271)	9	(229)	15° bevel on both edges
CC	1	drawer bottom	plywood	$\frac{1}{4}$	(6)	$10\frac{11}{16}$	(271)	9	(229)	15° bevel on both edges
DD	1	drawer bottom	plywood	$\frac{1}{4}$	(6)	$10\frac{11}{16}$	(271)	9	(229)	15° bevel on both edges
EE	1	drawer bottom	plywood	$\frac{1}{4}$	(6)	$10\frac{11}{16}$	(271)	9	(229)	15° bevel on both edges
FF	1	drawer bottom	plywood	$\frac{1}{4}$	(6)	$10\frac{11}{16}$	(271)	9	(229)	15° bevel on both edges
GG	10	drawer pulls	hardwood	$\frac{1}{2}$	(13)	$\frac{1}{2}$	(13)	1	(25)	15° miter on both ends

Tools needed

random-orbit electric sander

table saw

biscuit joiner

jointer

block plane

bench plane

60-, 100-, 120-, 150- and 220-grit sandpapers

No. 0000 steel wool

sanding block

Hardware & Supplies

spray or wipe-on lacquer

NOTE This cutting list is as accurate as I could make it. I recommend cutting out the two sides, top, back and bottom parts first and assembling the box before cutting any other parts. Then use the box as your template for the exact angles. There's a possibility that your final box dimensions will differ slightly from what I've shown. That's the nature of making projects like this one. Use this cutting list as a guide for keeping track of all the parts.

step one | The joint between the veneer sheets becomes almost invisible if the edges of the sheets are straight and square. Using a jointer plane and a shooting board is the traditional method of straightening the veneer sheet's edges. Here I'm using a metal straightedge to hold the sheets flat and secure.

step two | The first step to laying up the veneer sheets is to secure them edge-to-edge with small pieces of masking tape.

step three | Run a strip of masking tape the length of the veneer joint.

step four | I like to glue the edges of the veneer sheets together the same way you'd glue boards edge-to-edge. Using the tape on the joint as a hinge, open the joint and run a bead of glue along the edge of one veneer sheet.

step five | Fold the joint closed. The glue will squeeze out, letting you know that you've got the edge covered with glue.

step six | Wipe away the glue squeeze-out with a damp cloth and let the glue dry. It helps to put the veneer between a couple of objects that will hold the joint tightly. (The tape is still on the other side.)

step seven | When the glue has dried on the veneer sheets, you can remove the masking tape. The sheets are now glued together and are one larger sheet. Apply a level coat of glue to the substrate only. If you're laying up more than one set of veneered panels, put waxed paper between the panels. Clamp them in your veneer press and let the glue dry for 24 hours. My veneer press includes two benchtop horses and two, 1½"-thick (38mm) particleboard plates. The horses hold the plates flat and allow room for the clamps under the plates.

Veneer panels for the top and two sides. If possible, have the grain wrap around the box. This adds a nice visual element. Also, veneer two panels: one for the back and one for the drawer fronts. Cut the top and two side panels to size. Cut some strips of the same veneer you used for the top and sides. Turn on your iron to its highest heat setting. Apply a layer of wood glue to the front edge of a side panel (level the glue so it covers the entire edge as shown in the photo). White, yellow or brown wood glue works for this procedure.

Place the veneer strip on the edge of the panel. Place the iron on the veneer and heat up the glue. You'll see some steam coming from the glue — that's the moisture leaving the glue. Move the iron steadily along the edge of the panel. When the steam stops, remove the iron. The glue should cure. If not, reheat until it does. Keep the iron moving so you don't scorch the veneer. Repeat this procedure to cover the front and back edges of the top and two side panels.

After you set down the iron, pick up one of your sanding blocks and use the back side of it to run back and forth on the veneered edge. This secures the veneer in place and speeds the cooling process.

Using a smooth-cut file, trim the excess veneer from the edge of the panel. Hold the file at a slight angle to the face of the panel as shown. You can smooth the edge veneer down to the face veneer without scratching the face veneer. Don't be too aggressive or you could cut into the face veneer. Use 150-grit sandpaper to sand the edges smooth.

Set your biscuit joiner to cut a slot ¼" (6mm) on center from the adjustable fence on the joiner. (Cut a No. 0 slot.) I've got older biscuit joiner, so yours may not look like mine, but they all work the same way. Hold the joiner as shown to cut slots in the bottom inside of both of the side panels. Use the bevel on the bottom edge as your angle guide.

Cut the slots in the ends of the bottom panel as shown. Register the biscuit joiner's fence on the bottom of the bottom. Note the bevel on the edge of the bottom. Don't let the face of the joiner register on this bevel.

Cut some biscuit slots in the edges of the back and the inside of the two side and top panels. The back is located ⅛" (3mm) in from the back edges of the top and two side panels, and covers the back edge of the bottom panel. Glue box together.

Cut some ¼"-thick plywood (6mm) for the drawer guides. You'll need about 26" (660mm) running inches cut at 9⅛" (232mm) wide. Then set your table saw blade to 15°. Start with the bottom drawer guides and work your way up the box.

Use some of the same plywood you'll use for the drawer bottoms as spacers for fitting the drawer guides. Each of the spacers represents the location of a drawer bottom.

Glue the drawer guides inside the box. Use a spring clamp to hold one end of the guide and use a finish nail to hold the other end. Push the nail into the back of the box just far enough to hold the nail in place as you wedge it against the drawer guide.

There obviously isn't enough room inside the box for you to swing a hammer (unless you know some little elves), so use a dowel with a hole as a pusher for the finish nails.

Here's what the drawer guide glue-up looks like when all the guides are held in place with spacers, clamps and nails. (Perhaps something ready to launch into space.)

Cut and fit the drawer bottoms before cutting any other drawer parts. It can take a little trial and error to get just the right fit. The bottoms should fit snugly but you should still be able to easily move them in and out of the box. Take your time with this operation as it will determine if the drawers work smoothly or if they stick or rattle.

13

14

Cut out the drawer sides next. Then cut out the drawer backs. I test-fitted each set of sides and back in the box before gluing anything together. The drawer sides and back should fit into their respective openings with about 1/64" (.4mm) total clearance. Now you can glue the sides to the backs.

15

Glue the drawer sides/back assemblies to their respective bottoms exactly on center with each other. The front ends of the sides are held flush with the drawer bottom. Note the temporary brace to keep the sides properly spaced during glueup.

16

This is the ideal fit for the drawers. There is a small space between the sides and the guides. More importantly, there is less space between the edges of the bottoms and the sides of the box. Remember that the bottoms also guide the drawers in and out of the box and hold the drawers at the proper spacing to one another.

17

Glue the drawer fronts to the front edges of the sides and bottom of each drawer. The bottoms of the fronts are held flush to the bottoms of the drawers. The one exception is the bottom drawer. This drawer front covers the front of the bottom panel of the box so its front is held 1/2" (13mm) below the bottom of the drawer. Got that?

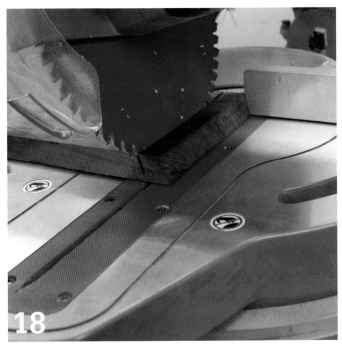

18

You can make drawer pulls from any wood you choose. I chose bubinga because it matches the rosewood veneer on the outside of the box and it contrasts nicely with the curly maple veneer on the drawer fronts. Set your table saw or miter saw to 15° and cut a couple of blanks for the drawer pulls. Cut these blanks cross-grain. Then, when you cut the pulls from these blanks, the grain will run the length of each pull.

19

The drawer pulls run centered along a line that radiates from the focal point of the extrapolated lines of the sides. (See the illustration to understand what I just said.) Configuring the pulls like this enhances the angular shape of the box and feet. After you've applied the finish and rubbed it out, lay the box on its back with the drawers installed. Mark the locations for the drawer pulls.

20

Mix up some two-part epoxy and put a small drop at each pull location. Set the pulls in the epoxy, easing them down flush with the drawer front.

21

Double-check the alignment of the pulls by sighting down from the top of the box. Your eye will tell you better than a ruler whether they are aligned properly. Let the epoxy cure completely before moving the box.

lookin' good

THIS BOX HAS A SPECIFIC PURPOSE — to keep jewelry safe and organized. The inside of the lid is fitted with a mirror. My version should have a mirror, but I broke it before I could get it mounted into the box. Oops. And, as the old saying goes, the show must go on, so the photo shoot went on. This box will be a gift for my daughter, and it will have a mirror when I give it to her.

I've always wanted to use red oak and wenge in the same project because they are opposites in color but they have the same open grain pattern. I had some padauk I thought would be good for the lid panel, so this turned into a colorful project. (The padauk will age to a deep burgundy color in about six months.)

The joinery in this box teaches you yet another way to make dovetails — using a router and a template. These dovetails look like they were cut by a machine and that's OK. It's honest, strong, quick-to-make joinery and the box will never come apart. If you were making a run of 20 or 30 drawers for a kitchen, this is the way you would make them.

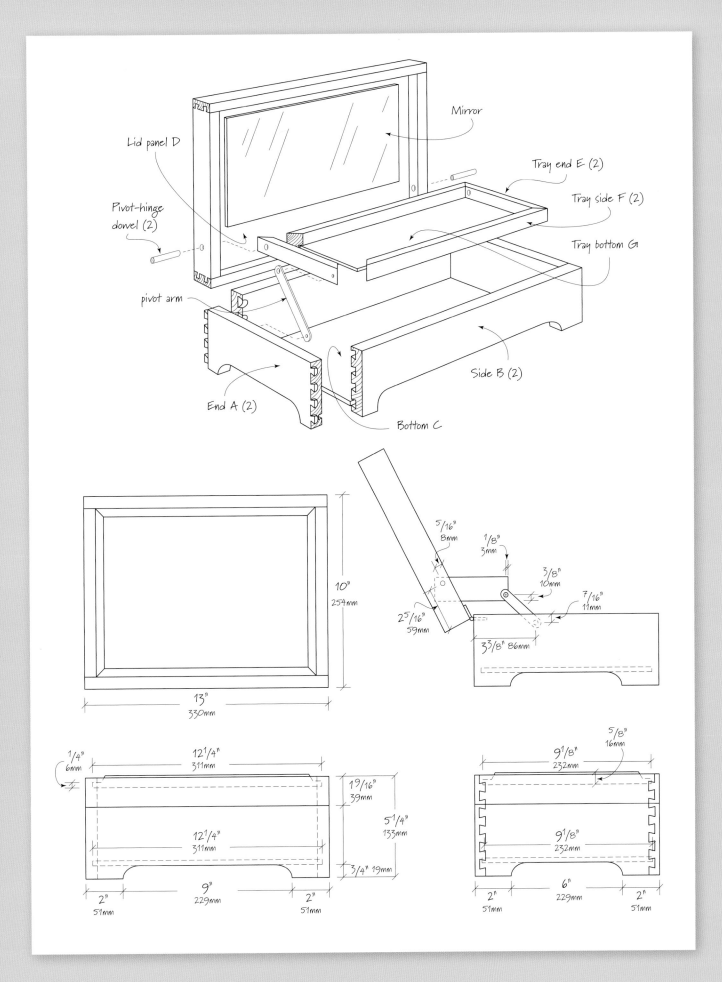

Mirror

Lid panel D

Pivot-hinge dowel (2)

pivot arm

End A (2)

Bottom C

Tray end E (2)

Tray side F (2)

Tray bottom G

Side B (2)

10"
254mm

13"
330mm

5/16"
8mm

1/8"
3mm

3/8"
10mm

7/16"
11mm

2 5/16"
59mm

3 3/8" 86mm

1/4"
6mm

12 1/4"
311mm

19/16"
39mm

5 1/4"
133mm

12 1/4"
311mm

3/4" 19mm

2"
51mm

9"
229mm

2"
51mm

5/8"
16mm

9 1/8"
232mm

9 1/8"
232mm

2"
51mm

6"
229mm

2"
51mm

inches (millimeters)

REFERENCE	QUANTITY	PART	STOCK	THICKNESS	(mm)	WIDTH	(mm)	LENGTH	(mm)
A	2	ends	red oak	⅝	(16)	5¼	(133)	9½	(241)
B	2	sides	wenge	⅝	(16)	5¼	(133)	13	(330)
C	1	bottom	plywood	¼	(6)	9¼	(235)	12¼	(311)
D	1	lid panel	padauk	⅝	(16)	9⅛	(232)	12¼	(311)
E	2	tray ends	red oak	¼	(6)	1¼	(32)	4	(102)
F	2	tray sides	red oak	¼	(6)	1¼	(32)	11¼	(286)
G	1	tray bottom	plywood	¼	(6)	3¾	(95)	11	(279)

Hardware & Supplies

1   1" x 11½" (25mm x 292mm) continuous hinge

1   ⅛" x ½" x 2¾" (3mm x 13mm x 70mm) pivot arm

1   6" x 11" (152mm x 279mm) mirror

spray or wipe-on lacquer

Tools needed

table saw

router

dovetailing jig

sanding block

random-orbit electric sander

stationary disc sander

oscillating-spindle sander

drill

screwdriver

60-, 100-, 120-, 150- and 220-grit sandpapers

No. 0000 steel wool

Dovetail template quick setup

Several different companies manufacture this type of dovetailing jig, but basically they all work the same way. The parts that receive the tails are held vertically and the parts that receive the sockets are held horizontally. At each end of the jig, there are stops that determine the offset of the vertical and horizontal parts. This makes it possible for you to rout the parts at the same time, ensuring that their top edges are flush when the parts are assembled. These stops are preset at the factory and need no adjustment.

NOTE Mark all box or drawer parts with a triangle on their top edges.
These top edges will always face to the outside of the dovetail routing jig.

step one | To set up the jig, hold a box end or drawer front/back under the finger plate at one end of the jig. Loosen the knobs that adjust the height of the finger plate and push the plate flat onto the part. Tighten the set screw at that end of the plate. Move the part to the other side of the plate and repeat. This sets the height of the finger plate.

step two | Insert a box or drawer side into the front of the jig behind the pressure bar. Hold the end of the part snugly against the underside of the finger plate and against the stop, and tighten the pressure bar. (Be sure the pressure bar is tightened evenly at both ends, otherwise the part could slip while you're routing.)

step three | Insert the box end or drawer front/back under the plate and push the end of the part firmly against the back of the box or drawer side. Tighten the pressure bar to hold the part securely in place.

The first step is to run the router right to left (the opposite direction for normal cutting) across the front of the vertical part and make a scoring cut. This will prevent tearout. When running the router in this direction, take care to make this a shallow cut; otherwise the router might grab onto the work and jump ahead unexpectedly. It's not dangerous, but it can surprise you if you're not expecting it.

1

2

Joints made using this jig are strong and clean looking. Make test-cuts using scrap pieces of wood to set up the jig and router. If you find the tails are a little too large to fit into the sockets, lower the base of the router slightly towards the tip of the router bit. If the tails are too small, raise the router base slightly away from the tip of the bit. This is a trial-and-error procedure, so be patient.

3

Cut the grooves for the bottom and top panels in the middle of a tail. The tail will hide the groove when the box is assembled. Cut the groove in the mating socket of the box end parts.

4

Mark where the feet will start and draw a line parallel to the bottom of the box, connecting these marks. I used a flat washer to draw the curve for the feet. It's about a 1" (25mm) radius.

5

Cut on the outside of the lines for the feet, leaving the pencil lines visible. Then set up a fence on your band saw that's ¾" (19mm) from the blade. Starting in the middle of the cutouts, push the part until the feet are against the fence and make the straight cut up to where the curve starts. Flip the part over and cut to the other foot. This is a nifty way to make the straight cuts straight.

6

Use an oscillating-spindle sander to true up the curves for the feet. You can also use a spindle sander on your drill press. Use light pressure when sanding these curves — you're sanding end grain and it can heat up quickly and burn.

7

Sand the curve until it blends with the straight line. Oops, even with light pressure, I made a small burn line!

You can use your router table or table saw to cut the profile on the lid panel. I have a router bit that cuts a small raising profile that's perfect for this box.

Sand the insides of the box sides and ends. Also, sand the lid panel. Dry assemble the box with the bottom and top panels in place to be sure everything is OK. If you're good to go, apply glue to the dovetails. You don't need to apply glue in the sockets.

Attach the two sides to one end, then insert the lid and bottom panels, then attach the other end panel. One of the cool things about dovetails cut with this jig: At assembly time you don't need to use clamps.

11

The bottom panel of the box is flush with the bottom of the cutout for the feet. Secure the bottom with some screws.

12

When the glue dries, cut the lid from the box. Center the cut on the space between the sockets and pins.

13

Cut the tray parts, then cut a rabbet in the bottom edges. Cut 45° miters on both ends of the end and side parts.

14

Tape the ends of the parts together, apply glue to the miters and fold the tray together.

15

Cut the bottom of the tray to size and glue it in place.

16

Set up two stop blocks and cut the mortise for the continuous hinge using a straight router bit.

17

I used a piece of flat steel bar for the pivot arm. As an alternative, you could use a piece of brass or aluminum. Drill and countersink the holes in the bar.

It took some trial and error to find the correct angle and location for the lift bar and pivot points between the tray and lid. Use the illustration to help you lay out these locations.

18

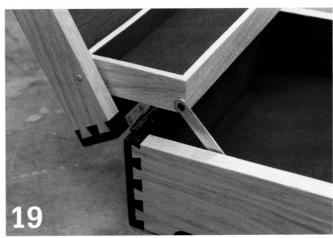

19

When the lid is opened, the tray will follow. The pivot arm acts as a stop for the lid. You want the tray to be level or parallel with the base of the box. After you've applied the finish to the box, lid and tray, apply flocking to the inside of the tray and the box. Then install the dowel hinges in the tray and attach the pivot arm to the tray and lid.

The wooden dowels protrude through the sides of the lid and add a visual feature that I thought was interesting.

20

18

cutting-edge display

IF YOU HAVE A COLLECTION OF KNIVES, thimbles or chrome-plated valve lifters, this project is for you. You can adapt it to suit your needs. The feature that makes this project neat is the custom cutouts made to fit each item in your collection.

I used straight-grained yellow pine for the box and frame. The straight grain doesn't draw attention to itself and lets the collection have the spotlight.

You'll learn how to make fitted panels for holding special items. You can use this technique to hold small or delicate tools in your toolbox drawers. The flocking applied to this project's fitted panel is necessary for keeping the collection safe, and the single color will set off the collection.

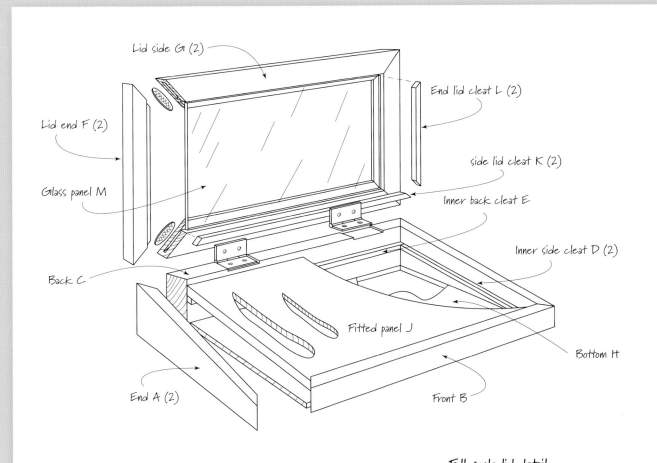

Lid side G (2)

End lid cleat L (2)

Lid end F (2)

side lid cleat K (2)

Glass panel M

Inner back cleat E

Back C

Inner side cleat D (2)

Fitted panel J

Bottom H

End A (2)

Front B

Full-scale lid detail

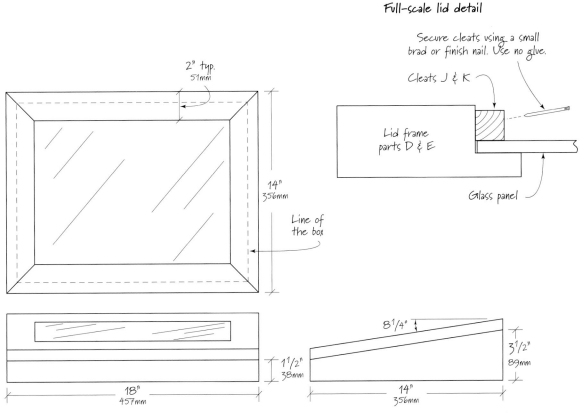

Secure cleats using a small brad or finish nail. Use no glue.

Cleats J & K

Lid frame parts D & E

Glass panel

2" typ.
51mm

14"
356mm

Line of the box

8 1/4°

3 1/2"
89mm

1 1/2"
38mm

18"
457mm

14"
356mm

inches (millimeters)

REFERENCE	QUANTITY	PART	STOCK	THICKNESS	(mm)	WIDTH	(mm)	LENGTH	(mm)
A	2	ends	yellow pine	3/4	(19)	3 1/2	(89)	14	(356)
B	1	front	yellow pine	3/4	(19)	1 1/2	(38)	18	(457)
C	1	back	yellow pine	3/4	(19)	3 1/2	(89)	18	(457)
D	2	inner side cleats	yellow pine	1/2	(13)	1/2	(13)	12	(305)
E	1	inner back cleat	yellow pine	1/8	(3)	1/2	(13)	16 1/2	(419)
F	2	lid ends	yellow pine	3/4	(19)	1 1/2	(38)	14	(356)
G	2	lid sides	yellow pine	3/4	(19)	1 1/2	(38)	18	(457)
H	1	bottom	plywood	1/4	(6)	13 1/2	(343)	17 1/2	(445)
I	1	fitted panel	plywood	1/2	(13)	10	(254)	13	(330)
J	1	backer board	plywood	1/4	(6)	13 1/2	(343)	17 1/2	(445)
K	2	side lid cleats	yellow pine	5/16	(8)	5/16	(8)	16	(406)
L	2	end lid cleats	yellow pine	5/16	(8)	5/16	(8)	12	(305)
M	1	glass panel	glass	1/8	(3)	12	(305)	16	(406)

Tools needed

table saw

band saw

jigsaw

dovetail saw

chisels

sanding block

random-orbit electric sander

stationary sander

60-, 100-, 120-, 150- and 220-grit sandpapers

No. 0000 steel wool

Hardware & Supplies

1   1 1/4" x 1" (32mm x 25mm) butt hinges

spray or wipe-on lacquer

Lay out the sides first. Use the illustration as a starting point for proportions and adjust them according to your particular needs. The angle of the slope isn't that critical. The measurements at the front and back of the sides will determine the angle. The rest of the parts will be measured using the sides.

Rough-cut the angles on the sides. Use a hand plane or jointer to straighten the saw cut. Make sure the two side pieces are exactly the same size.

Stand the side on its top edge and set the table-saw blade to the end angle. This is the bevel angle for the top edges of the front and back box parts.

4 Use the side part as a template and mark the height of the front and back parts. Then cut the bevel on the parts.

5 Cut the 45° miters on the ends of all the box parts. Then cut a rabbet (for the bottom part) in the bottom edge of all the parts.

6 Tape and glue the miter joints and fold the box together. Cut the bottom panel to size and glue and screw it in place.

7 Cut the lid parts to size, cut the miters on the ends and cut biscuit slots in the miters.

8

Cut a rabbet on the inside edges of the lid parts, then glue the frame together. Rest the frame on two clamps and straddle the frame with two more clamps. Tighten the clamps until the joints are all tight and square.

9

While the glue is drying on the lid frame, cut three cleats and glue them in place inside the box. Rest the front ends of the two side cleats on the bottom of the box and raise the back end of the cleat so the cleat is parallel to the top edge of the sides. Glue the cleat to the back of the box flush with the top ends of the side cleats.

10

Cut the inner panel to fit inside and rest on the cleats. Arrange your collection on the panel and trace around each piece.

11

When you cut out the traced shapes, cut on the pencil line so it disappears. Then the cutout will be just the right size and the pieces should easily fit into the openings. If not, use a rasp to adjust the fit of the cutout. Then, using sandpaper, smooth the insides of the cutouts and the edges.

12

Glue the backer board to the back of the fitted panel. Apply glue sparingly between the cutouts so the glue doesn't squeeze out into the cutouts.

Cut the mortises for the hinges and install the hinges on the box.

13

14

Install the glass in the lid. Attach the lid to the hinges using one screw in each hinge. Close the lid to be sure that it lines up with the box. Make the necessary adjustments. When the lid is properly aligned, install the remaining hinge screws.

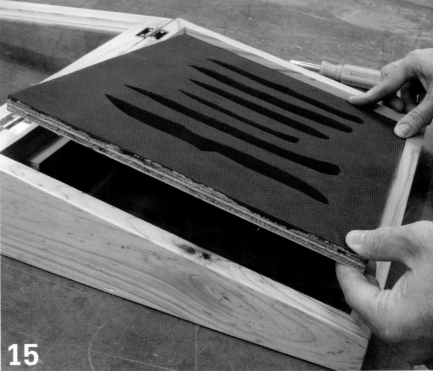

15

Finish the box and apply flocking to the fitted panel. When all is dry, simply drop the panel in place and you're good to go.

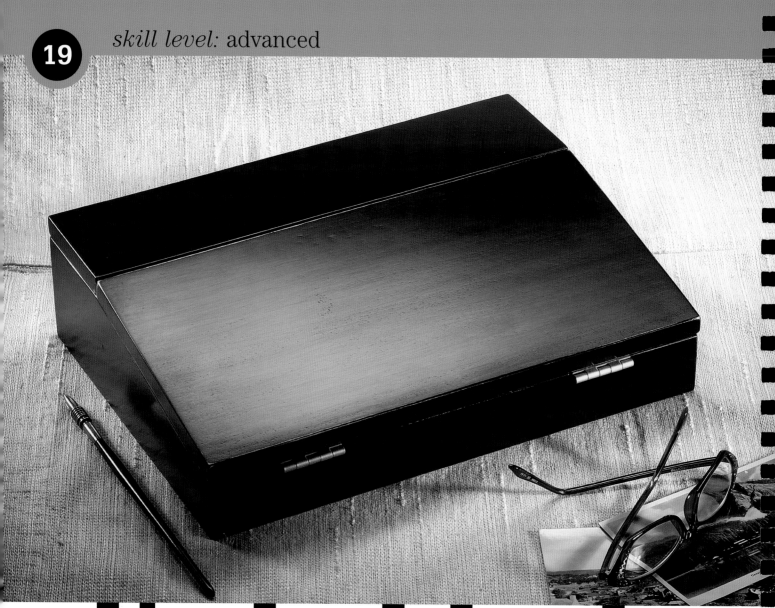

little black box

THE LAP DESK was a common item in the early 1800s. I saw this project in a book about country furniture. The original had two dividers in the tray section that created inkwell storage. I eliminated those and raised the bottom of the storage section so the box could accommodate larger sheets of paper. If you prefer, there is another lid that you can make to cover the inside of the box (see the illustration). It's hinged on the inside front of the box.

Here you'll learn about using dadoes in case construc-tion, opening the door to some groovy projects. A rail, shelf or partition that is housed in a dado and glued and/or screwed or nailed in place can be used to build strong bookcases, kitchen cabinets, dressers and of course — boxes.

The careful planning and lay out of dadoes is the most im-portant rule. Once you've cut a dado, you're totally committed.

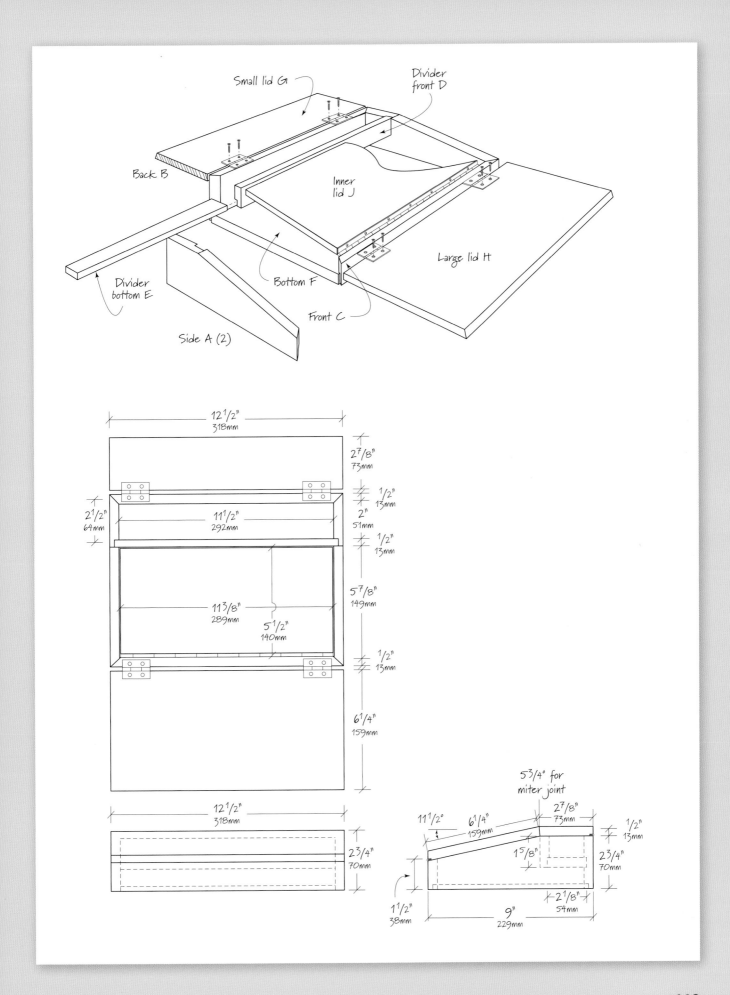

Small lid G

Divider front D

Back B

Inner lid J

Large lid H

Divider bottom E

Bottom F

Front C

Side A (2)

12 1/2"
318mm

2 7/8"
73mm

1/2"
13mm

2 1/2"
64mm

11 1/2"
292mm

2"
51mm

1/2"
13mm

11 3/8"
289mm

5 1/2"
140mm

5 7/8"
149mm

1/2"
13mm

6 1/4"
159mm

12 1/2"
318mm

2 3/4"
70mm

5 3/4° for miter joint

11 1/2°

6 1/4"
159mm

2 7/8"
73mm

1/2"
13mm

1 5/8"

2 3/4"
70mm

1 1/2"
38mm

9"
229mm

2 1/8"
54mm

119

inches (millimeters)

REFERENCE	QUANTITY	PART	STOCK	THICKNESS	(mm)	WIDTH	(mm)	LENGTH	(mm)
A	2	sides	poplar	3/8	(10)	2 3/4	(70)	9	(229)
B	1	back	poplar	3/8	(10)	2 3/4	(70)	12 1/2	(318)
C	1	front	poplar	3/8	(10)	1 1/2	(38)	12 1/2	(318)
D	1	divider front	poplar	3/8	(10)	1 5/8	(41)	11 3/4	(298)
E	1	divider bottom	poplar	3/8	(10)	2 3/8	(60)	11 3/4	(298)
F	1	bottom	poplar	1/4	(6)	8 1/2	(216)	12	(305)
G	1	small lid	poplar	3/8	(10)	2 3/8	(60)	12 1/2	(318)
H	1	large lid	poplar	3/8	(10)	7	(178)	12 1/2	(318)
I	1	inner lid	poplar	3/8	(10)	5 5/8	(143)	11 3/8	(289)

Tools needed

table saw
jointer
router table
sanding block
block plane
bench plane
random-orbit electric sander
60-, 100-, 120-, 150- and 220-grit sandpapers
No. 0000 steel wool

Hardware & Supplies

2 sets	1" x 1 1/2" (25mm x 38mm) butt hinges
1	1" x 11 1/2" (25mm x 292mm) continuous hinge
spray or wipe-on lacquer	

Cutting the parts for this project is similar to the "Cutting-Edge Display" project. After you're finished cutting the parts, lay out the dadoes and cut them using a 3/8" (10mm) router bit in your router table. Then cut a rabbet in the bottom inside edge of the box front, back and sides. See the illustration for details on dado locations.

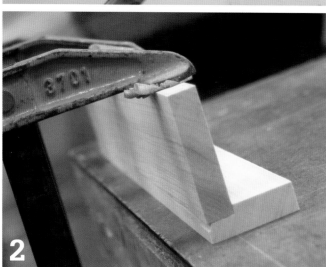

Glue the divider bottom to the divider front.

Glue the two sides, back, divider front, divider bottom and the front (not shown).

Cut the bottom to size and glue and screw it in place.

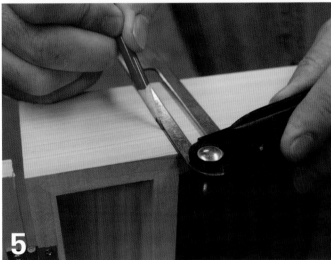

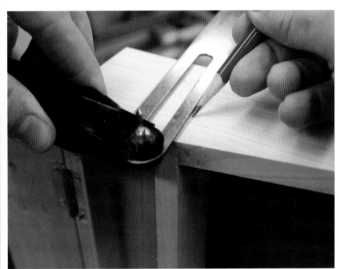

The small and large lids have miters cut on the two edges that come together on the top of the box. Cut the tops to fit the box. To find the miter angle of two panels that meet at a nonstandard angle (standard angles are 22½°, 30°, 45°), set your sliding T-bevel to an angle that looks close to what the miter angle would be. Draw a line as shown in the first photo. Then flip the sliding T-bevel over and compare the angle to the one you just drew. If it's not the same, adjust the T-bevel a little, erase the first line and repeat the procedure. When the two angles are the same, that's your miter angle. Use the T-bevel to set the angle on your table saw.

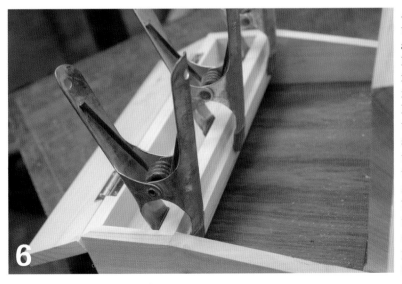

After cutting and fitting the two outside lids, use white, yellow or brown wood glue to attach faux leather to the inside top of the large outside lid. If you choose to make the inner lid, cut it to fit the space between the front and the divider front, and glue faux leather to its top. Lay out and cut the mortises for the hinges that attach the two outside lids to the box. Use a continuous hinge to attach the inner lid and install a cleat on the front of the divider front (it will act as a stop for the lid). Install the inner lid so it sits below the top edge of the end panels. This is to account for the thickness of the two pieces of faux leather so the outer lid will close properly. For painting and finishing details, see the chapter "Is It Finished Yet?"

old-school laptop

BACK IN THE DAY when people wrote with quill pens and ink-wells, they also used this type of lap desk when they traveled. In this updated version, I've included compartments for storing stationary, envelopes, pencils, pens, stamps and a candle (just in case the electricity goes out).

It's my hope that this project will promote handwritten letters. It's still a treat to receive a letter in the mail!

This project calls for a veneered surface. Veneering is a great way to use exotic or burl wood at a fraction of the cost of the hardwood equivalent.

You don't want this laptop to be heavy to carry around, so use a lightweight wood such as pine, mahogany or walnut. The writing surface is covered with a faux leather material that costs a fraction of the price of real leather — and you can buy it by the lineal yard to make dozens of these laptops if you're feeling energetic.

Be sure to make at least one for yourself, then write some letters or make a journal entry.

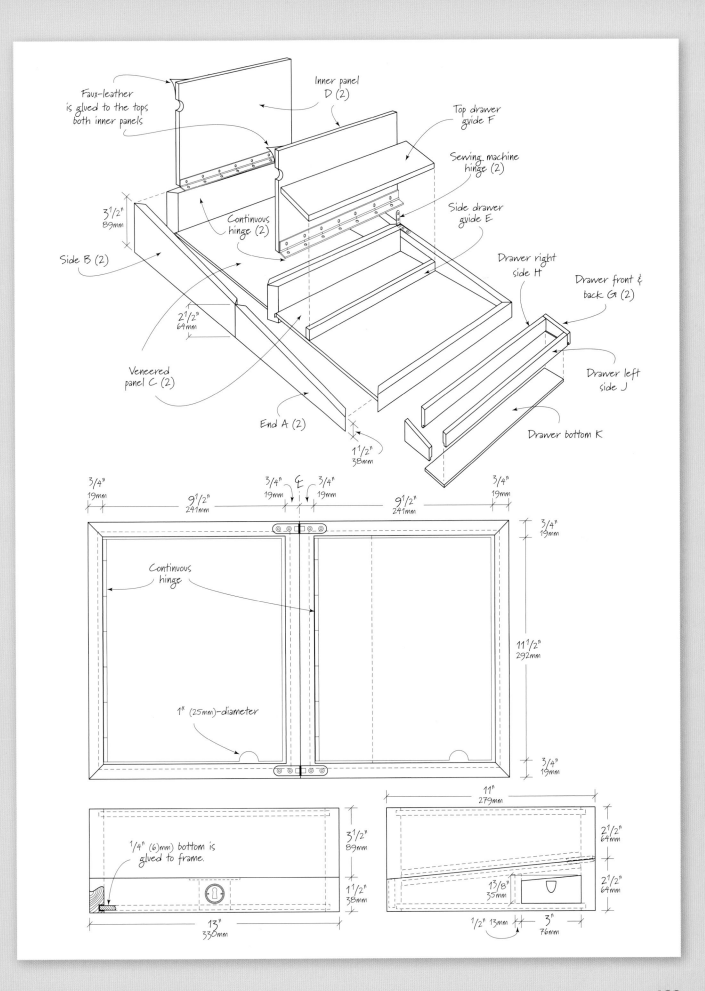

Faux-leather is glued to the tops both inner panels

Inner panel D (2)

Top drawer guide F

Sewing machine hinge (2)

Side drawer guide E

3 1/2" 89mm

Side B (2)

Continuous hinge (2)

Drawer right side H

Drawer front & back G (2)

2 1/2" 64mm

Veneered panel C (2)

Drawer left side J

Drawer bottom K

End A (2)

1 1/2" 38mm

3/4" 19mm

3/4" 19mm   ₵   3/4" 19mm

9 1/2" 241mm

9 1/2" 241mm

3/4" 19mm

3/4" 19mm

Continuous hinge

11 1/2" 292mm

1" (25mm)-diameter

3/4" 19mm

1/4" (6mm) bottom is glued to frame.

3 1/2" 89mm

1 1/2" 38mm

13" 330mm

11" 279mm

2 1/2" 64mm

13/8" 35mm

2 1/2" 64mm

1/2" 13mm

3" 76mm

inches (millimeters)

REFERENCE	QUANTITY	PART	STOCK	THICKNESS	(mm)	WIDTH	(mm)	LENGTH	(mm)
A	2	ends	mahogany	3/4	(19)	5	(127)	11	(279)
B	2	sides	mahogany	3/4	(19)	5	(127)	13	(330)
C	2	veneered panels	plywood	1/4	(6)	10	(254)	12	(305)
D	2	inner panels	plywood	1/2	(13)	9$\frac{7}{16}$	(240)	11$\frac{7}{16}$	(291)
E	1	side drawer guide	mahogany	1/2	(13)	1$\frac{1}{8}$	(29)	11$\frac{1}{2}$	(292)
F	1	top drawer guide	mahogany	1/2	(13)	3$\frac{3}{4}$	(95)	11$\frac{1}{2}$	(292)
G	2	drawer front/back	mahogany	1/2	(13)	1$\frac{3}{8}$	(35)	3	(76)
H	1	right drawer side	mahogany	1/2	(13)	1$\frac{3}{8}$	(35)	10$\frac{1}{2}$	(267)
I	1	left drawer side	mahogany	1/2	(13)	1$\frac{1}{4}$	(32)	10$\frac{1}{2}$	(267)
J	1	drawer bottom	hardboard	1/8	(3)	2$\frac{1}{2}$	(64)	11	(279)

Tools needed

table saw
miter saw
drill press
jointer
sanding block
block plane
bench plane
random-orbit electric sander
stationary sander
60-, 100-, 120-, 150- and 220-grit sandpapers
No. 0000 steel wool

Hardware & Supplies

2 sets	sewing machine hinges, Rockler #30879
1	full mortise lock, Rockler #33432
1	1$\frac{1}{4}$" x 11$\frac{1}{2}$" (32mm x 292mm) continuous hinge

spray or wipe-on lacquer

Veneers are cut into flitches, which means they're sliced along the length of the log and stacked just as they were when the log was whole. You will typically buy part of a flitch. To create a bookmatched pattern, one sheet of veneer is flipped or turned over like a page in a book and placed edge-to-edge to the next sheet. I used rosewood veneer for the veneered panels. When I placed the sheets next to each other (as shown in the photo), I thought the grain pattern created too much of a tapered look.

I restacked the sheets and, using a straightedge as a guide, I cut the veneer more parallel to the grain.

When the veneers were bookmatched, the grain pattern flowed better (at least to my eye). The dark curvy grain at the bottom of the veneers will be cut away when the panels are cut to size. (See sidebar on page 99 for gluing veneers.)

4

Cut the side and end parts to size and cut the 45° miters on the ends of all the parts. Cut the side parts into angled halves. To make a fixture that holds the side parts at the proper angle, lay out the shape of the bottom half of the side and cut out that shape in a scrap of wood. Use it as shown. One side will be cut with miters facing up, the other will be cut with the miters facing down. Hold the bottom edge of both parts against the fixture.

5

Measure the angle on the end of a side. Set the table saw blade to this angle.

6

Use an end to mark the height of the front and back bottom halves. Cut out these parts on the table saw with the blade set to the angle from step 5.

7

Cut the veneered panels to size. Cut the grooves for these panels in the box parts. Then glue the top and bottom box sections together. Use glue to hold the panels in place to add strength to the box sections. Use the router table to cut the mortises for the hinges and install the hinges.

8

Cut the box compartment parts and glue them inside the lower box section. Cut out and glue the drawer parts together and fit the drawer. The hole for the drawer locking pin must be in line with the side of the drawer.

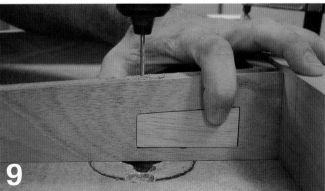

9

Close the drawer and drill the hole through the box side into the drawer side.

10

Drill the hole for the threaded brass insert that guides and keeps the spring-loaded locking pin in place. This hole is drilled to the depth of the insert.

11

To cut the fingernail drawer pull, clamp the drawer at an angle against the drill press fence and cut the notch using a ⅝" (16mm) Forstner bit.

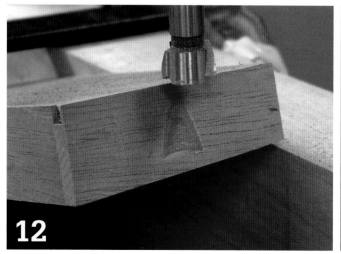

12

Stop the cut ¼" (6mm) from the top of the drawer. I used a gouge and removed more of the wood in the cutout and left the tool marks. It gave the the fingernail pull some texture.

13

Use a Forstner bit to cut the shallow mortise for the lock's mounting plate.

14

Then reset the drill press depth of cut and make the mortise for the body of the lock. This is a great way to cut mortises using just your drill press and some Forstner bits!

15

Mark the location of the keyhole using the lock's cover plate as a template.

Cut the keyhole using a drill bit and a sharp knife.

Cut the inner panels to fit inside the box section and glue the faux leather to the outsides of the panels (see sidebar, page 99). Cut the finger pull in the inner lids using a 1½" (38mm) Forstner bit. A Forstner bit cuts the outside of the hole as well as removing material inside the hole, so it's the best choice for cutting half of a hole.

I lined the box and drawer with felt. After you've applied the finish to the box, cut the felt to size. Then spread a layer of white, yellow or brown carpenter's glue on all the areas where you'll be applying the felt.

Press the felt into place. The glue will start setting right away, so get the felt in place quickly. Finally, install the lock, attach the cover plate over the keyhole, install the box hinges and install both inner panels using continuous hinges. If you like, you can use a couple of small magnetic catches to hold the inner lids in place.

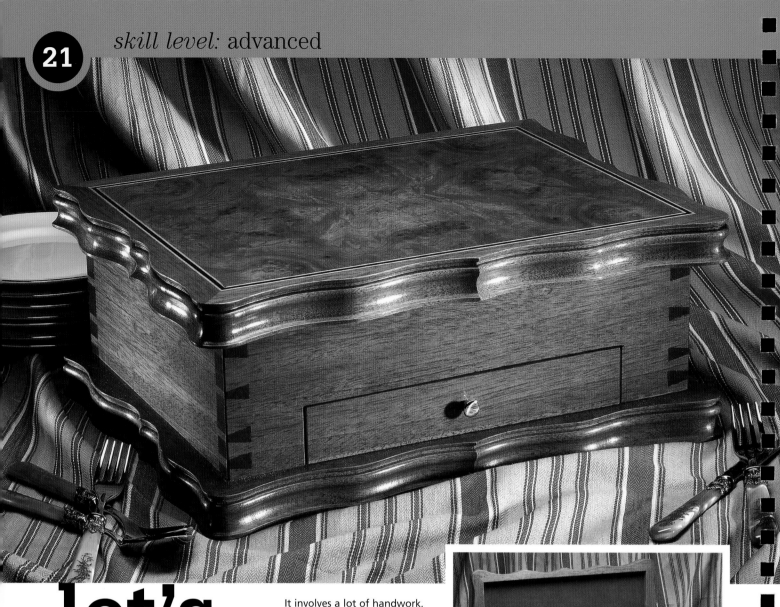

let's eat

HEY, WHEN DO WE EAT?
Get the table set, then we can
eat...

You won't keep your every-
day flatware in this box but it
is the right place for the good
stuff. This box keeps the silver
safe and ready to use when the
need arises.

This is probably the most
complex project in this book.

It involves a lot of handwork,
along with power tools. But
like everything else in woodworking, this project is built
following a series of steps that
in and of themselves are not
complicated.

You learned about veneer-
ing in previous projects: This
one will show you how to
match and lay up burl veneers.
You'll also get to cut some
dovetails using hand tools. The
scrollwork on the lid and bottom is an exercise in cutting
curves and routing along those
curves. It's fun!

The final finish on this project is more work than the other
projects. I talk about it in the
last chapter. Suffice it to say

that you'll get an aerobic work-
out when completing the finish.

Then it will definitely be
time to eat!

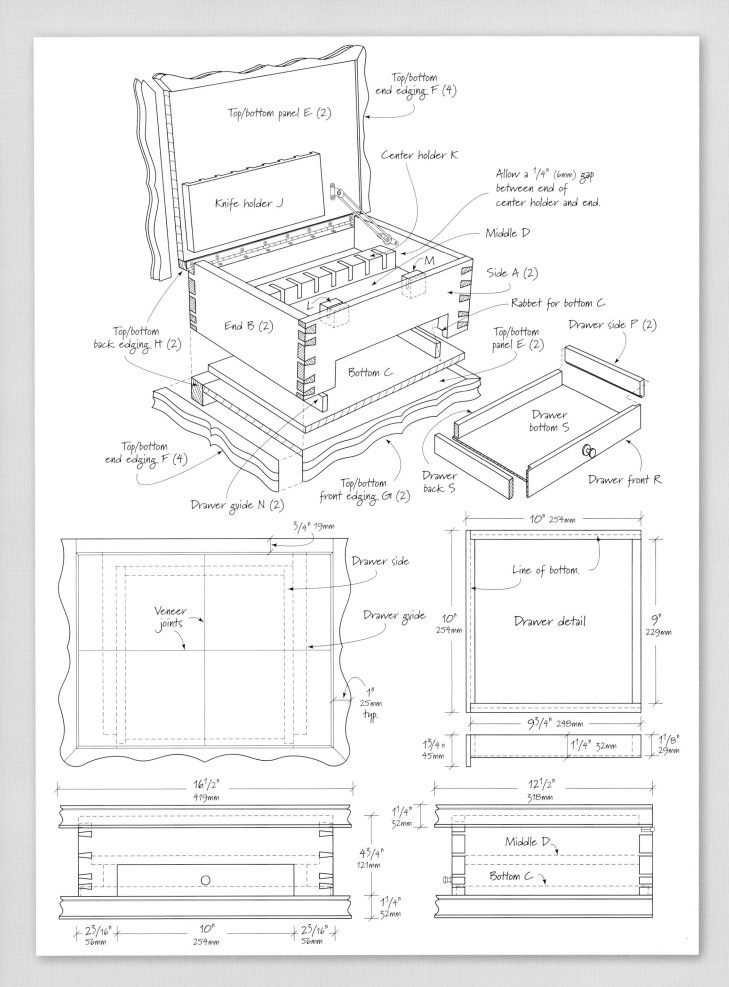

Top/bottom end edging F (4)

Top/bottom panel E (2)

Center holder K

Allow a 1/4" (6mm) gap between end of center holder and end.

Knife holder J

Middle D

M

Side A (2)

Rabbet for bottom C

Drawer side P (2)

Top/bottom back edging H (2)

End B (2)

L

Top/bottom panel E (2)

Bottom C

Drawer bottom S

Top/bottom end edging F (4)

Drawer guide N (2)

Top/bottom front edging G (2)

Drawer back S

Drawer front R

3/4" 19mm

Drawer side

10" 254mm

Veneer joints

Drawer guide

Line of bottom.

10" 254mm

Drawer detail

9" 229mm

1" 25mm typ.

9 3/4" 248mm

1 3/4" 45mm

1 1/4" 32mm

1 1/8" 29mm

16 1/2" 419mm

1 1/4" 32mm

12 1/2" 318mm

4 3/4" 121mm

Middle D

Bottom C

1 1/4" 32mm

2 3/16" 56mm

10" 254mm

2 3/16" 56mm

129

inches (millimeters)

REFERENCE	QUANTITY	PART	STOCK	THICKNESS	(mm)	WIDTH	(mm)	LENGTH	(mm)	
A	2	sides	mahogany	3/4	(19)	4 3/4	(121)	14 3/8	(365)	
B	2	ends	mahogany	3/4	(19)	4 3/4	(121)	11 1/2	(292)	
C	1	bottom	plywood	1/2	(13)	11	(279)	14 1/8	(359)	
D	1	middle	plywood	1/2	(13)	10	(254)	12 7/8	(327)	
E	2	top/bottom panels	plywood	1/2	(13)	10 13/16	(275)	14 1/2	(368)	veneer top panel
F	4	top/bottom end edging	mahogany	1	(25)	1 1/4	(32)	12 1/2	(318)	
G	2	top/bottom front edging	mahogany	1	(25)	1 1/4	(32)	16 1/2	(419)	
H	2	top/bottom back edging	mahogany	3/4	(19)	1 1/4	(32)	14 1/2	(368)	
J	1	knife holder	plywood	1/2	(13)	4	(102)	11	(279)	
K	1	center holder	poplar	1 1/4	(32)	1 1/2	(38)	12 5/8	(321)	
L	1	long front holder	poplar	1 1/4	(32)	1 1/2	(38)	2 5/8	(67)	
M	1	short front holder	poplar	1 1/4	(32)	1 1/2	(38)	2	(51)	
N	2	drawer guides	poplar	3/4	(19)	1 1/4	(32)	10	(254)	
P	2	drawer sides	mahogany	1/2	(13)	1 1/4	(32)	9 3/4	(248)	
Q	1	drawer back	mahogany	1/2	(13)	1 1/8	(29)	9	(229)	
R	1	drawer front	mahogany	1/2	(13)	1 3/4	(44)	10	(254)	
S	1	drawer bottom	plywood	1/4	(6)	9 1/2	(241)	9 3/4	(248)	
T		inlay strip		1/16	(2)	1/4	(6)	54	(1372)	running inches

Tools needed
table saw
router table
dovetail handsaw
chisels
sliding T-bevel
screwdriver
drill
twist drill
sanding block plane
random-orbit electric sander
stationary sander
60-, 100-, 120-, 150- and 220-grit sandpapers
No. 0000 steel wool

Hardware & Supplies
1   14 3/8" (365mm) continuous hinge
1   lid stay
1   1/2" (13mm) brass knob
spray or wipe-on lacquer

After cutting the sides and ends to dimensions, set your marking gauge to the thickness of the parts.

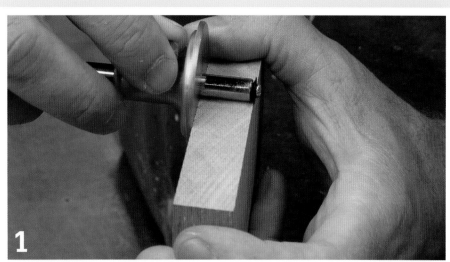

Score a line on the ends of the end parts. This scored line is where you'll stop the dovetail pin cuts.

3

Lay out the pins using your sliding T-bevel and a ruler. It's traditional to make the pins narrow. Space them however you like. I put the two outside pins closer together. Cut on the outside of the lines that mark the pins and cut down to your scored line. Be sure to mark the waste material between the pins.

4

It's easier for me to make all the cuts on the same side of each pin, then make the cuts on the other side of each pin. That way, I only change the angle of the saw two times.

5

Remove the material between the pins. Clamp the part to a scrap board and start chiseling. Some woodworkers like to use a coping saw or band saw to remove the bulk of the material, then clean up using a chisel. I never trusted myself doing it that way, so I stick with the mallet and chisel. Try it both ways and see what you like the best. There's no magic bullet to this process. Keep practicing using your chisel and mallet and you'll soon get a feel for it.

6

Use the pins as a template and, using a sharp pencil, mark the tails on the sides. Note the numbers on each part. Each set of pins is probably a little different (because they're hand-cut), so be sure to mark each set of pins and matching tails.

7

Cut the tails down to the scored line. Cut on the outside of the tail marks. Again, remember to mark the waste between the tails. After you've cut the tails, remove the material between them as you did for the pins.

8

Hopefully the joints fit together. You may need to trim the inside of the tails just a little to get a snug fit. What's a snug fit? It varies with the density of the wood you're using. For mahogany, the joint can be a little snug and still go together because the wood is soft and will give a little. If you're using maple, however, the joints need to be cut precisely. Maple will not forgive imperfections. (That's why I like softer woods for making hand-cut dovetails.) Once you're a pro, use all the maple you want.

step one | If veneer has been stored in a dry place and/or has been around for awhile, it has a tendency to dry out. When this happens with burl veneer, it becomes like the Appalachian Mountains — lots of hills and valleys. If you were to put this into a press, the veneer would scream for mercy and crack up. I use a spray bottle with water in it to spritz a mist over the veneer. Do this with each sheet of veneer that you're going to use.

step two | When all the veneer sheets are damp, layer them in your press with three or four sheets of newspaper between each sheet of veneer. The newspaper will absorb the excess water and help disperse the moisture evenly throughout the sheets of veneer. Apply enough pressure on the press to squeeze the veneers flat and leave the press alone for at least 24 hours. Then release the clamps and check the veneer. If it is still quite damp, replace yesterday's damp newspaper with today's news. Retighten the clamps and give it another 24 hours, then check again. You want the newspaper and veneer to be almost dry or, at most, slightly moist. The veneer will feel cool to the touch. This means the veneer is happy and you've been successful in rehydrating it. It will gladly bend, not crack or break.

9

10

Glue the box sides and ends together. Let the glue dry, then rout the bottom panel. I used a rabbeting bit, which is made especially for this kind of cut. It won't tear or splinter the wood.

What is this, cutting in the middle of the front? Yup. I wanted the drawer front to match the piece from which it's cut, and this handsaw has a small kerf that ensures the drawer front will fit nicely in the cutout. This is called a plunge cut because you start the cut on the surface of the wood and work your way down.

11

Make the vertical cuts squarely to the edge of the front using a combination square.

12

I left the rounded corners in the rabbets and fitted the bottom to the cut. Glue the bottom in place. Then cut the drawer guides and glue them inside the box. The edges of the guides should be flush with the ends of the drawer-front cutout and square to the front of the box.

13

Cut the drawer parts to length and slightly wider than shown in the cutting list. Then fit the sides to the drawer opening so they slide in and out smoothly. Cut the back to the same width as the sides minus the thickness of the bottom. Cut a rabbet in the bottom inside of the drawer front so it fits over the front edge of the box's bottom. This rabbet needs to include the thickness of the drawer bottom. Cut rabbets in the drawer sides for the drawer bottom. Cut the drawer bottom and glue the drawer together.

14

Cut the notches in the center holder using a dado head in your table saw. If you don't have a dado cutter, use your router table with a straight router bit. I used different sized spacers to locate the notches. Or, you could simply move the saw's fence after making the cuts at each end of the part. Move it the same distance each time and you're good to go. Make the two front holders from a long piece of wood, cut the notches, then cut the parts to length.

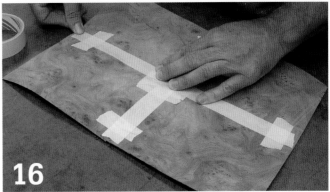

16

If necessary, flatten the burl veneers (see sidebar, "Flattening Veneer" on the previous page). Cut four consecutive pieces of veneer to one-quarter the size of the top panel. Joint two adjacent edges to exactly 90°. Flip two veneers over (like opening a book), then flip up a single veneer from each set like you're opening a briefcase. This is a four-way book-match. The 90° corners should all come together perfectly; unless you're dead accurate, you'll need to do a little tweaking of the joints. That's OK. A hair's-width removal of material won't be noticed. Tape the joints together and glue them as shown in the sidebar, "Preparing Veneers for Layup" in chapter 16.

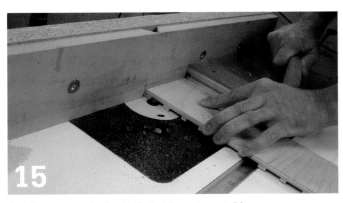

15

Cut the grooves in the knife holder using a table saw or, as shown here, a router table. I chose the router table because it cuts plywood cleanly.

17

Remove the tape from the veneer joints after the glue has dried and lay up the top panel in your press.

18

When the panel has been in the press for 24 hours, remove it. From the middle of the panel, where the joints converge, measure half the length and width of the finished dimensions of the panel and draw a mark. Do this both ways on the panel and cut the panel to your marks. This is the surefire way to get the veneers centered on the panel.

19

Use a straight bit and your router table to cut the rabbet for the inlay strips. Make the rabbets slightly less deep than the thickness of the inlay. After the inlay is glued in place, it will be easy to level it to the veneer.

20

Mark each inlay strip to length using the panel as your guide.

21

Miter cut the ends of the inlay strips.

22

Tape each strip in place and fit the next one to it. Then remove the tape, add glue to the rabbet and tape the strips back in place. Place the panel in your veneer press for 1 hour. Then remove the panel from the press, remove the tape and carefully hand sand the inlay strips level with the veneer.

23

24

Mill the edging to size, miter the ends and glue them to the top and bottom panels. Attach the back edging (not shown in the photo) first, then the front edging, then cut and fit the end edgings. Hold the edgings as close to flush as possible to the surface of the veneer or just slightly proud of the veneer. Do not let the top of the edgings get below the surface of the veneer. You'll end up sanding through the veneer trying to level the edging to the veneer. I've found that using blocks cut to precise thickness and placed under the panel is an easy way to keep the edging level to the panel.

Gently clamp the edging to the panel. No undue clamping pressure is necessary — ever. If you have to apply excessive clamping pressure, you need to check and fix your joinery. No amount of pressure will make it right — you'll end up ruining your clamps

25

26

Make a full-scale layout of the scalloping on the top and bottom panels' edges. Then apply the patterns with spray adhesive. Cut the patterns using a band saw or jigsaw. Sand the scalloping to final shape, removing any saw blade marks.

Cutting this profile is easily done using your router table and a router bit. I recommend you purchase a router bit that has the profile you like so you can perform this operation in one step. You will find many uses for this router bit.

27

Using your table saw, cut a $^{13}/_{16}$"-deep (21mm) by $^{7}/_{8}$"-high (22mm) rabbet in the top back of the box. The dimensions of this rabbet are determined by the thickness and height (add the thickness of the continuous hinge to the height) of the top back edging. Adding $^{1}/_{16}$" (2mm) to the depth of the rabbet gives clearance for the lid to be closed.

28

Cutting the rabbet in step 27 makes it possible for the back of the lid to be flush with the back of the box and the back of the bottom. It also makes it possible for the lid to close around the top of the box, creating a mild seal which helps to slow down the tarnishing of the silver flatware.

is it finished yet?

ONCE YOU'VE BUILT YOUR PRICELESS BOX, YOU
NEED TO FINISH IT. (This is where a lot of folks get
discouraged because they've had not-so-good experi-
ences in the past when it came to finishing.)

The fear of finishing wood is real. A lot of woodworkers build furniture and then hire a professional to finish
their work. That's a viable option. (We used a professional finishing shop for years at a particular cabinet
shop.) The finishers were set up to do finishing and
nothing else. They produced a great-looking finish while
we concentrated on building a great-looking project.

However, finishers need to make a living too, and
they charge accordingly for their services. I'd like to
show you how you can achieve a better than average
(and in some cases, professional) finish that holds up
to scrutiny from the harshest critics.

Does finishing take a lot of time? Am I (the woodworker) truly able to apply a professional-looking
finish? No and yes to the questions. Let's get started.
I've taken the finishing demonstrations you'll use for
several of the projects in this book and put them into
one chapter. This is the final step — make it a good one.

one | **grain coloring**

Some types of wood such as oak, ash and mahogany have open pores that you can fill with color to make an interesting finish. There are a couple of easy ways to do this. One is to simply paint the wood after it's been finish-sanded. Let the paint dry, then sand the wood again until you remove as much of the paint as you like. Then apply a clear top coat of lacquer or polyurethane, depending on what type of paint you've used. Polyurethane can be used as a top coat over anything. Lacquer can be used to top coat only lacquer-based paints.

You can use oil-based or water-based paint for coloring the grain. You can also use colored lacquer, but it dries too quickly to make it practical for all but the smallest surfaces. When the paint has dried, sand it until just the right amount remains in the grain for your particular needs. After all, it's your project.

Another way to achieve this finish is to apply a sealer to the wood first. A sealer will seal the wood just a little. It does so by getting its little sealer hands into the open pores of the wood and setting up house. That way, nothing else can get in there. When the sealer dries, sand it smooth using 320-grit sandpaper. Then apply a thinned coat of paint and wipe it off immediately. Some of the color will stay behind. You can control the amount of color you want using this method. Try both methods to see how it works.

This is the final look of the "Big Top" box. I wanted just the deepest parts of the oak to retain the color. For a more colored look, you could use the method in step three and leave more of the paint on the wood.

OK, there are a couple of types of painted surfaces — those that are done with a brush and those that are sprayed. I like to spray because it doesn't leave brush marks, the coverage is even and it's quicker.

Because I painted the "Crazy 20" project, I used two-part auto body putty and drywall spackling to fill the edges of the plywood and to fill any voids in the joints or dings in the plywood. The auto body putty is like epoxy — you mix a little hardener with the putty and it's ready to go. It will dry quickly and forms a hard filler that you can sand, shape and paint. The drywall spackling is best for filling the small dings, dents and little voids. It also dries quickly and is easily sanded and painted.

Sand and shape the filler, working up to 220-grit sandpaper. Apply a coat of primer. What's great about primer is that it has a lot of solids in it. That means it will build up to a thick coat that can be sanded. After you apply a couple of coats, sand it using 320-grit sandpaper and you will achieve an amazingly smooth surface. If any dings remain, you can fill them with spackling, sand and apply more primer, then sand the primer. Keep doing this until you like the way the surface looks.

Apply the paint. It will flow so smoothly you'll be amazed. Until you've prepared a surface using this method, you don't truly understand how smooth a finish can be. Apply another coat of paint if needed. You can stop here if you like, but take it to the next level. Shall we? You bet! Apply a clear top coat. Be sure the clear top coat won't wrinkle or react with the paint. Try it out on a test piece to be sure.

This is the final finish on the "Crazy 20" box. I did all the steps as outlined above. The key to this type of painted finish is how smooth you can make the surface before painting. Finish-sanding the wood's surface using 220-grit sandpaper is sufficient. The filling, sanding with 320 grit, filling, sanding, priming, sanding, priming and sanding will fill any small scratches the 220-grit sandpaper leaves behind. When the paint touches the smooth surface, it's a happy occasion — for you and the paint. For the final and ultimate touch, you can wet sand the clear top coat with 600-grit wet/dry sandpaper. Then rub out the finish using No. 0000 steel wool. A final coat of wax will leave all who behold this finish breathless. For more on the wet-sanding process, see "Wet Sanding, Not Sanding Wet."

three | a primer primmer

You must use a primer that is compatible with the paint or lacquer you'll be using. If you don't apply primer, there is a good chance the paint won't cure properly. I was finishing a tabletop that I had made of MDF. After I shaped and sanded the top, I applied the colored finish lacquer. The lacquer wouldn't cure and remained soft, even after I waited several days. I had to remove the finish and use the recommended primer first. When the finish lacquer was applied over the primer, it cured to a nice hard finish. Lesson learned the hard way.

four | stain isn't necessarily a pain

As a general rule, I don't like to use stain. I prefer, like many woodworkers, to see the natural color of wood. Most wood changes color over time and it's something that makes wood, well, wood.

I did apply stain to one of the projects in this book. The "Let's Eat" project is made of mahogany. Mahogany turns a deep orange-brown over time, and I wanted just a little more brown in the final color, so I applied a medium-brown gel stain that brought out the end grain of the dovetails and added depth to the color of the carpathian elm burl veneer on the box's lid. This was one time that using stain made the project that much richer in color and texture.

five | textured paint isn't rough to use

The "Safely Kept" project is painted. It differs slightly from the painted finish on the "Crazy 20" box in that it calls for textured paint. The "Safely Kept" bank is made of MDF. I shaped and finish-sanded it using 220-grit sandpaper. I applied primer and sanded using 220-grit sandpaper. A couple of coats of primer were all that was needed. The textured paint came straight out of a spray can. I sprayed it on the project, and it worked its magic right in front of my eyes! It looks like hammered steel. I applied one more coat to ensure even color coverage and that was that.

The textured paint on the "Safely Kept" project added an element of realism. I finished the tumbler knobs with spray-on gloss enamel paint. A dab of red paint served as orientation indicators for the tumbler knobs.

six | **wet sanding, not sanding wet**

The first time I ever wet sanded a project, I was confused. Wasn't lacquer allergic to water? And here I was using water to wet sand a freshly lacquered tabletop. (Actually the lacquer had been curing for a week.)

That's the first thing to remember — let the lacquer cure for at least a week, even more if you have time. Lacquer will shrink in its first few days of being in the world. Then it settles down to live life one day at a time. If you're planning on wet sanding, you should have 10 to 15 good, even coats of lacquer on the surface. Lacquer blends with itself, so every time you apply another coat, it essentially becomes one thicker coat. And so it goes coat after coat.

The reason for wet sanding is to level the little hills and valleys in the lacquer. Use 600-grit wet/dry sandpaper to do the trick. I use water and a few drops of liquid dishwashing soap. The soap helps the sandpaper glide better. The water keeps the sandpaper lubricated and clean so it can cut through the surface of the lacquer. Dip the sandpaper in the water and drip some water on the surface to be sanded. Start sanding, occasionally adding water so the surface stays wet.

As you're sanding, the surface of the lacquer will start to dull. These are the hills being leveled. There will be places where it stays shiny. Those are the valleys. You want to keep sanding until the whole surface becomes dull. This means you're done.

Check your progress frequently so

you don't sand through the lacquer! If you do sand through, you'll need to stop sanding and reapply more coats of lacquer. If you sand through the lacquer on veneer, it's possible the veneer could absorb the water and buckle. Trust me, it's happened. So avoid sanding through the lacquer!

seven | **the rub out**

When you've successfully wet sanded your project to a wonderfully smooth lacquer finish, you're ready to rub it with No. 0000 steel wool. Unroll the steel wool bale and make it fit your hand. Rub completely from one end of the surface to the other.

Be careful not to get the lacquer too warm or it will start to melt. Take it easy and pay attention to the warmth of your hand. Also, take care at the edges and sharp corners. These areas don't have much lacquer on them, so you could rub through. How do I know about all these mistakes? I've made them, so hopefully you won't!

When the surface is shiny and even, you're done. As the final finishing touch, apply some paste or liquid wax to the surface. Let the wax dry a little, then rub it shiny. Wow, I can see myself!

eight | **polish it off**

I wet sanded the "Let's Eat" project. Veneers that have been carefully laid up like this deserve the very best. A lacquer finish with a wet-sanded surface that has been steel-wool rubbed and waxed encourages the beauty of the wood to shine through and protects it in the process. The veneer is happy, the lacquer is happy and best of all, you're happy with a job well done.

nine | **making new look old**

The "Little Black Box" is a painted project I chose to give a used look. When the paint was dry, I used No. 0000 steel wool to rub out the finish — literally. Steel wool removes finish much the same way hands and fingers wear away the finish over time. It doesn't take much rubbing to remove the paint, so proceed slowly and you'll do fine.

ten | **three cheers for lacquer**

It's time for me to reveal the finishing for the boxes in this book: I painted two, I wet-sanded and polished one, I shellacked one and the rest I finished with precatalyzed nitrocellulose lacquer. Precatalyzed lacquer doesn't require the use of a sanding-sealer primer. It acts as its own sealer. It also cures harder than traditional nitrocellulose lacquer, but it has all the positive working characteristics of nitrocellulose lacquer — namely, it will dissolve and blend with any previous layers of lacquer and you can easily wet sand without having to worry about sanding through to the next layer of finish. (This will happen if you try to wet sand or level polyurethane finish.)

I've set up a small spray booth in my garage with a tube-axial fan made especially for spray booths. It doesn't spark and it creates good air flow. I can purchase precatalyzed lacquer at my local paint store in a flat, satin or gloss finish. It

also comes in colors, which is a great way to paint. Lacquer is highly flammable but with adequate ventilation it's safe to use and it dries quickly — usually in 15 to 30 minutes.

I finish-sanded all projects using 220-grit sandpaper to remove all tooling and coarser-grit sandpaper marks. I then sprayed one coat of lacquer on the project. I let this dry, sanded it using 320-grit sandpaper and applied a second coat of lacquer. That's it.

I let the second coat of lacquer dry for several days before sanding it one more time with 320-grit sandpaper. I rubbed out each project with No. 0000 steel wool, then applied a coat of wax. Wax helps keep the lacquer surface free of fingerprints and further protects from moisture. If at anytime you want to remove wax, wet a rag with mineral spirits and rub the surface clean. Mineral spirits will not dissolve or harm lacquer.

suppliers

ADAMS & KENNEDY — THE WOOD SOURCE
6178 Mitch Owen Road
P.O. Box 700
Manotick, Ontario
Canada K4M 1A6
613-822-6800
www.wood-source.com
Wood supply

ADJUSTABLE CLAMP COMPANY
417 North Ashland Avenue
Chicago, Illinois 60622
312-666-0640
www.adjustableclamp.com
Clamps and woodworking tools

B&Q
B&Q Head Office
Portswood House
1 Hampshire Corporate Park
Chandlers Ford
Eastleigh
Hampshire SO53 3YX
0870 0101 006
www.diy.com
Woodworking tools, supplies and hardware

CONSTANTINES WOOD CENTER OF FLORIDA
1040 East Oakland Park Boulevard
Fort Lauderdale, Florida 33334
800-443-9667
www.constintines.com
Tools, woods, veneers, hardware

FRANK PAXTON LUMBER COMPANY
5701 West 66th Street
Chicago, Illinois 60638
800-323-2203
www.wwhardware.com
Wood, hardware, tools, books

THE HOME DEPOT
2455 Paces Ferry Road
Atlanta, Beorgia 30339
800-553-3199 (U.S.)
800-668-2266 (Canada)
www.homedepot.com
Woodworking tools, supplies and hardware

LEE VALLEY TOOLS LTD.
P.O. Box 1780
Ogdensburg, New York 13669-6780
800-871-8158 (U.S.)
800-267-8767 (Canada)
www.leevalley.com
Woodworking tools and hardware

LOWE'S HOME IMPROVEMENT WAREHOUSE
P.O. Box 1111
North Wilkesboro, North Carolina 28656
800-445-6937
www.lowes.com
Woodworking tools, supplies and hardware

ROCKLER WOODWORKING AND HARDWARE
4365 Willow Drive
Medina, Minnesota 55340
800-279-4441
www.rockler.com
Woodworking tools, hardware and books

TOOL TREND LTD.
140 Snow Boulevard
Concord, Ontario
Canada L4K 4C1
416-663-8665
Woodworking tools and hardware

TREND MACHINERY & CUTTING TOOLS LTD.
Odhams Trading Estate
St. Albans Road
Watford
Hertfordshire, U.K.
WD24 7TR
01923 224657
www.trendmachinery.co.uk
Woodworking tools and hardware

VAUGHAN & BUSHNELL MFG. CO.
11414 Maple Avenue
Hebron, Illinois 60034
815-648-2446
www.vaughanmfg.com
Hammers and other tools

WOODCRAFT
P.O. Box 1686
Parkersburg, West Virginia 26102-1686
800-535-4482
www.woodcraft.com
Woodworking hardware

WOODWORKER'S HARDWARE
P.O. Box 180
Sauk Rapids, Minnesota 56379-0180
800-383-0130
www.wwhardware.com
Woodworking hardware

WOODWORKER'S SUPPLY
1108 North Glenn Road
Casper, Wyoming 82601
800-645-9292
Woodworking tools and accessoried, finishing supplies, books and plans

index

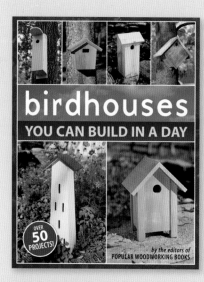

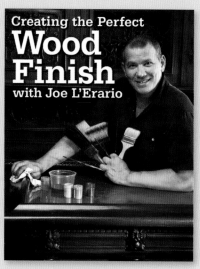